THE STEEL STRIKE OF 1919

THE STEEL STRIKE OF 1919

EDITED WITH AN INTRODUCTION BY

Colston E. Warne

AMHERST COLLEGE

Problems in American Civilization

D. C. HEATH AND COMPANY
A division of RAYTHEON EDUCATION COMPANY
LEXINGTON, MASSACHUSETTS

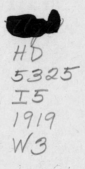
COPYRIGHT 1963 BY D. C. HEATH AND COMPANY

PRINTED IN THE UNITED STATES OF AMERICA

PRINTED AUGUST 1968

INTRODUCTION

ONE of the major convulsions in American labor history was the Steel Strike of 1919 which, for a period, badly crippled the iron and steel industry. This strike pitted the leadership of a war-expanded and highly integrated industry against a coordinating committee of craft unions affiliated with the American Federation of Labor. The strike ended in the complete defeat of the unions after unprecedented losses to both sides, not to mention the cost to the nation as a whole. Viewed from the standpoint of organized labor, giant autocratic corporations had triumphed through espionage, blacklists, the denial of freedom of speech and assembly, and through their complete unwillingness to recognize the right to collective bargaining with representatives of the workers' own choosing. Viewed from the standpoint of the corporations, the strike represented the handiwork of radicals and professional labor agitators who had secured the uncomprehending adherence of a minority of foreign-born and largely unskilled steel laborers. It did not arise out of dissatisfaction with existing wages, hours, or working conditions but from the actions of those who wished to impose the closed shop upon a dynamic industry.

Tensions in the steel industry had mounted during World War I. Organized labor had grown in strength and prestige during the course of the war. The Chicago leadership of the American Federation of Labor had just concluded the successful organization of packinghouse workers and in 1919 felt the time ripe for a test of strength in steel. The unions, in launching the strike, stressed two major demands: (1) Union recognition was necessary in order to provide a democratic channel through which grievances might be handled, and (2) a contract should be signed with the participating unions which would both improve wages and bring about the abolition of the 12-hour workday.

The American labor movement which in 1919 challenged this citadel of American industrialism had first gained firm roots in the 1850's in such crafts as the typographers, the molders, and the carpenters. By fixing standards of apprenticeship, standards of skill, and common standards of wages for a craft, these early unions developed a fraternal spirit as well as the economic power to withstand employer opposition. Collective bargaining agreements were formulated which stipulated the wages, the hours, and the working conditions in each craft or trade. While such agreements often broke down in periods of depression, by the 1880's a sufficiently strong nucleus of craft organizations had developed so that a central federation emerged. This was the American Federation of Labor, headed by Samuel Gompers, a leader in the Cigar-makers' Union.

The ideas of the A.F. of L. reflected in substantial measure the personality of Gompers who, as his ideas matured, stoutly repudiated socialism and advocated a pragmatic, "pure and simple" unionism which accented trade agreements with employers — agreements which would spell out for a stipulated period the wages, the hours of work, and the procedures for the handling of grievances. Gompers believed that Labor had most to gain by organizing in crafts and by making and keeping firm economic bargains. His accent was thus on the organization of skilled workers. Under his leadership, the Federation made substantial though intermittent progress, although its exclusive craft emphasis was, in time, somewhat amended. In 1892, the Federation's affiliate in the steel industry lost its substantial footing among the skilled workers in the Carnegie Steel Mills of Pittsburgh. Following the bitter Homestead strike of that year, Andrew Carnegie and H. C. Frick were able to clear the way for the open-shop policy which the United States Steel Corporation was to enunciate just after the turn of the century.

The struggle at Homestead was, however, but one in a series of bitter industrial battles which featured the last quarter of the 19th century. Unionism sought persistently to secure and retain a foothold in such major industries as railways, steel, mining, and building. Railways proved sufficiently vulnerable so that the major independent operating crafts were in that period able to secure collective bargains on most lines. The Debs attempt to consolidate these gains into a unified industrial union, the American Railway Union, collapsed, however, in the Pullman Boycott of 1894.

The miners proved sturdy and persistent unionists. Departing from Gompers' formula, they merged their crafts into the United Mine Workers of America, an industrial union which admitted to membership all those working in and about a mine, whether skilled or unskilled. This organization, after a series of costly strikes, entrenched itself in the Northern bituminous mine fields at the turn of the century and shortly thereafter in anthracite. Affiliated with the A.F.

of L., the United Mine Workers thus became an industrial union in a federation composed largely of craft organizations. It was, however, in the building trades, where the craft principle was most dominant, that the American Federation of Labor steadily developed its largest single membership component. These groups were conservative in outlook and aristocratic in behavior. They possessed unity and substantial bargaining power.

The Federation under Gompers' guidance sought to conciliate American bankers and industrialists who had become fearful of a tide of radicalism. Socialist forces led by De Leon and Debs were clamoring for government ownership of the trusts. The syndicalists of the Industrial Workers of the World (I.W.W.), formed in 1905, clamored for "one big union" to oust "the ruling class" and demolish the wage system. In this setting, business leadership was badly divided. To some, the wise course was that of striking down organized labor of whatever type as an enemy to "the American way of life." This meant the employment of injunctions which would paralyze the right to strike by court action. It also meant espionage and the denial of the right of assembly. To more conciliatory business leaders, a moderate policy seemed appropriate. Samuel Gompers' offer of cooperation appeared a good substitute for the class struggle.

As this confusion of counsel persisted, the election of Woodrow Wilson in 1912 held out hope of freedom from the injunctive restraints which had hampered union growth. The period also brought forward a number of new unions in areas which had previously been featured by immigrant sweatshops. Chief among these were the International Ladies' Garment Workers Union, an A.F. of L. affiliate, and the Amalgamated Clothing Workers Union, an independent industrial union. These organizations served as vivid reminders that the new immigrants could be effectively organized.

As trade unionism gained ground prior to World War I, a new countervailing force was also set into action by industrialists. Employee representation plans were established in mines and factories in a "company union" movement. Such plans varied widely from company to company but normally gave an outlet for the handling of grievances and included welfare activities. The most notable plan of this type was that of the Colorado Fuel and Iron Company, a Rockefeller corporation which had experienced an especially bitter strike. This plan represented an about-face in the personnel policy of the company and was heralded by its authors as establishing a new era in which management and the duly-elected representatives of its employees would sit down with a mutuality of interest.

To Samuel Gompers these company unions were frauds. The only acceptable agency for collective bargaining was for him the trade union which would represent craftsmen employed not in a single company but in many concerns. The object of unionism was, Gompers felt, to establish a wage level which would not be competitively undercut by nonunion workers. To attain bargaining strength, Gompers proposed that agreements contain clauses stipulating that an employer hire only union men (the closed shop); or at least that any person employed should subsequently be compelled to join a union (union shop). Where the labor movement was weak, however, he was willing to accept lesser compromises. Employers, on the other hand, advocated

what they called the open shop — by which they typically meant a shop in which any worker, union or nonunion, might be employed and one which did not engage in collective bargaining. Unionists countered by alleging that in such shops discharge was the almost inevitable fate of the active unionist.

America's participation in World War I gave the American Federation of Labor new prestige and importance. Samuel Gompers endorsed the war wholeheartedly. In return, he was accorded a measure of recognition both in the war administration and at the Peace Conference. At the same time, the war weakened some enemies of the Federation and created others. The I.W.W., which had attained strength, particularly in the West, opposed the war and was crushed with patriotic fervor. Debs was jailed for a pacifist speech. Many of those who had sympathized with syndicalism or with socialism came to repudiate their earlier faith. Yet in the fall of 1917 the October Russian Revolution triggered off a new force which was to have powerful repercussions upon American labor. In its initial impact, it served to fragment the left-wing into quarreling groups. Yet, to employers, Bolshevism seemed both a real and a powerful menace. A violent distrust of the foreign-born and of dissident ideas emerged, which led to the Palmer Raids on radicals and to attacks on free speech.

This fear of the spread of Bolshevism has a special relevance to the problem of the Steel Strike of 1919 since it did much to color the attitude of employers in this dispute. The strike was initially generated in Chicago by the Chicago Federation of Labor. The head of that federation, John Fitzpatrick, while never personally a radical, was thought by industrialists to have been susceptible to radical influences. The chief target of employers was, however, William Z. Foster, a lieutenant of Fitzpatrick's, who had repudiated his earlier strong championship of the syndicalist policies of the I.W.W. and had been welcomed back into the American Federation of Labor by Samuel Gompers. To the steel executives, this was but a boring-from-within tactic, employed to gain a foothold within industry, awaiting the day of final radical triumph.

Both in Europe and in the United States deep stirrings had been felt in labor circles at the war's conclusion in November 1918. Prices had greatly increased, generally more rapidly than wages. Unionists felt the time propitious for a militant drive to extend collective bargaining. In Labor circles, Wilsonian democracy was interpreted as implying a new arena for democratic action—the democratization of the job by establishing the right of workers to elect representatives of their own choosing to meet with employers. To industrialists the time was at hand for the end of "silk shirt extravagance" and for a true return to normalcy. A pivotal clash between these forces was the Steel Strike of 1919.

Providing a background for the conflict are the initial readings on the rise of integration in the steel industry drawn from Walter Adams: *The Structure of American Industry*. In this selection, Adams competently shows how the United States Steel Corporation had placed itself in a position where it could both unify price policies and extend its effective cooperation with other companies into the labor field. These policies were not without their impact upon the outcome of the strike.

Conflicting interpretations of the events leading to the conflict are given by William Z. Foster and Arundel Cotter. The basic philosophies of the parties to the dispute next appear in selections by Elbert H. Gary, Chairman of the United States Steel Corporation and spokesman for the companies, by John Fitzpatrick, chairman of the Strike Coordinating Committee, and by Samuel Gompers, head of the A.F. of L. Judge Gary's strong stand against recognizing affiliates of the American Federation of Labor or any other labor organization found general approval throughout the industry. The steel corporations of the time prided themselves upon their welfare programs, proclaimed the generosity of their wages, and found no room for trade unions in their plants.

Fortunately in the study of this problem we have, in addition to partisan statements issued by the contestants, the conclusions reached by two major investigating groups—the Senate Committee on Education and Labor and the Interchurch World Movement. Some highlights from the testimony and findings of these investigations are included. The Interchurch World Movement, led by Bishop Francis J. McConnell of the Methodist Episcopal Church, had, in its effort to mediate the dispute, established a committee of injuiry which included prominent members of the following denominations: Methodist, Baptist, United Evangelical, Disciples, Presbyterian, Congregational, United Brethren, and Protestant Episcopal. The Senate Committee on Education and Labor was chaired by Senator William S. Kenyon.

These two investigations reached quite different conclusions concerning the central issues in the strike. The Senate Committee expressed its concern over radicalism among the strike leaders and indicated its regret that President Wilson's request to postpone the dispute had not been heeded. In the main, it contented itself with the outlining of the issues between the contestants, as it saw them. This report brought a sharp retort from William Z. Foster who, in his book: *The Great Steel Strike and its Lessons,* took the opportunity to castigate the Committee as well as the steel companies. The Interchurch World Report firmly backed the unions' demand for collective bargaining. Because it was both couched in strong terms and reflected a unique ecclesiastical undertaking, it attracted widespread attention and widespread criticism. The United States Steel Corporation widely distributed a 475-page volume by Marshall Olds, which charged that the Interchurch Report was biased and that its research staff was dominated by radicals. Excerpts from Mr. Olds' *Analysis of the Interchurch World Movement Report on the Steel Strike* are included in the readings.

In a dispute as complex as the 1919 Steel Strike, many significant questions might be raised. Perhaps the central one is this: Was the strike a part of a radical conspiracy which employed violence to attain anti-American goals or was it a movement seeking laudable objectives in peaceful ways? In seeking to answer this question, one must face up to certain other issues: Were the companies justified in contending that individual workers were adequately protected without recourse to trade unions? Or were the steel workers entitled to collective bargaining through independent organizations? Were the steel workers in genuine protest against the 12-hour day or was the strike an excuse to get the company to pay a 12-hour wage for eight hours' work?

It is interesting to note that the 12-hour day in steel was abandoned in 1923 after an appeal by President Harding. Unionism in steel did not, however, again become significant until the mid-thirties when the reinvigoration of the United Mine Workers and other unions by the New Deal brought renewed demands for steel organization. Following internal conflicts within the American Federation of Labor, the Committee for Industrial Organization (C.I.O.) was formed in late 1935 by John L. Lewis of the United Mine Workers and other dissident A.F. of L. leaders. Expelled from the Federation, the C.I.O. launched a steel organizing drive in 1936, featured by Lewis' attempt to gain the allegiance of leaders of a company union which the U.S. Steel Corporation had tardily initiated.

To the surprise of the nation, conversations in the Spring of 1937 between Lewis and Myron Taylor of U.S. Steel resulted in a collective bargaining agreement between the Corporation and the C.I.O. affiliate. The spread of steel unionism to other companies came, however, only with the aid of the National Labor Relations Board and after protracted strikes, notably in Chicago. Today most of the industry is organized by the United Steel Workers (AFL-CIO) in a modified union shop.

The current position of unionism in steel does extreme violence to the principles so ably enunciated by the late Judge Gary. Some observers have maintained that the willingness of "Big Steel" to sign with Lewis was initially prompted by the presence of a New Deal administration and by the possibility of obtaining large government contracts in the late thirties. (Collective bargaining relations to the steel industry since 1937 have, indeed, been marked both by substantial government participation in labor relations and by large government steel purchases.)

This altered pattern of labor relations in steel lends additional interest to the stormy events of 1919. In the light of present-day trends, one is led to reflect again whether Gary and his colleagues were correct in "holding the line" against the development of mass labor organization in steel. This policy, if firmly maintained by his successors, might have limited the expansion of trade unions, which have become so powerful a factor in our economy. "As steel goes, so goes the nation" is an old adage which contains a considerable measure of truth. Equally, one is led to consider whether Foster, Fitzpatrick, and Gompers were merely ahead of their time in their unsuccessful attempt to organize this pivotal mass production industry as a counterpoise against giant aggregations of capital.

CONTENTS

1 WALTER ADAMS
   The Steel Industry 1

2 ARUNDEL COTTER
   United States Steel—A Corporation with a Soul 4

3 WILLIAM Z. FOSTER
   The Great Steel Strike and Its Lessons 12

4 ELBERT H. GARY
   Principles and Policies of the United States Steel Corporation 27

5 ELBERT H. GARY
   Testimony before the Senate Investigating Committee 33

6 SAMUEL GOMPERS
   Testimony before the Senate Investigating Committee 41

7 JOHN FITZPATRICK
   Testimony before the Senate Investigating Committee 50

8 PUBLIC OPINION AND THE STEEL STRIKE
   The Advertising Campaign 54
   Letter of Reverend Thomas Devlin 55

9 TESTIMONY OF RESIDENTS OF MILL TOWNS
   J. S. Oursler, General Manager of the Homestead Steel Works 58
   Reverend Adelbert Kazincy 59
   T. J. Davies 61
   Matt O'Reilly 65
   John J. Martin 66
   George Mikulvich 69

10 CONCLUSIONS OF THE SENATE COMMITTEE INVESTIGATING THE
   STRIKE IN THE STEEL INDUSTRIES 71

11 WILLIAM Z. FOSTER
    Analysis of the Senate Committee Report   81

12 CONCLUSIONS AND RECOMMENDATIONS OF INTERCHURCH WORLD   86
    MOVEMENT REPORT

13 MARSHALL OLDS
    Analysis of the Interchurch World Movement Report   102

    Suggestions for Additional Reading   108

CHRONOLOGY OF STRIKE

June 1918	Resolution is adopted at American Federation of Labor Convention at St. Paul, Minn., to launch a drive to organize the steel industry.
August 1, 2, 1918	Twenty-four unions meet in Chicago to form the National Committee for Organizing Iron and Steel Workers.
August–October 1918	Preliminary organizing attempts are made in Chicago and Gary, Indiana, area.
October 1918	Steel organizing is extended to Pittsburgh area, meeting with stubborn resistance.
May 15, 1919	Amalgamated Assn. of Iron, Steel and Tin Workers convention in Louisville writes Judge Gary asking for meeting to discuss organization. Request refused on May 20th.
June 20, 1919	Samuel Gompers, President of A.F. of L., writes Judge E. H. Gary asking conference to avoid industrial strife. His letter was not answered.
July 20–August 20, 1919	Members of affiliated unions in steel industry ballot on strike issue.
August 20, 1919	The 24 unions report a 98% vote in favor of a strike (100,000 voting).
August 26, 1919	John Fitzpatrick and his coordinating committee call at the office of Judge Gary to seek a conference.
August 27, 1919	Judge Gary refuses a conference, affirming that the unions do not represent a majority of steel workers and that the United States Steel Corporation follows an open shop policy. Union repeats request, suggesting that all issues be brought to joint conference.
September 7–9, 1919	President Wilson unsuccessfully seeks to bring the parties together in conference.
September 10, 1919	President Wilson urges postponement of strike until conclusion of industrial conference in Washington.
September 12, 1919	John Fitzpatrick refuses indefinite postponement, stating it would mean "absolute demoralization and utter ruin of our movement."
September 22, 1919	Strike begins.
September 23, 1919	U.S. Senate authorizes investigation of steel strike. Hearings open on September 25th in Washington, D.C., before Senate Committee on Education and Labor.
October 6, 1919	Industrial Conference called by President Wilson convenes in Washington.
November 28– December 5, 1919	Interchurch World Movement unsuccessfully seeks to mediate the dispute.
January 5, 1920	Strike is called off by participating unions.
June 28, 1920	Interchurch World Movement Report is adopted.

THE HIGH COST OF LOAFING
—Morgan in the Philadelphia Inquirer

THE NEW FREEDOM
—Walker in the New York Call (Socialist)

The Clash of Issues

We stand firmly on the proposition that industry must be allowed to proceed untrammeled by the dictates of labor unions or anyone else except the employer and the employees and the government. That is where we stand.

JUDGE E. H. GARY

There is one thing that must be understood, that the time has come when the workers have a better understanding of their rights in the industrial, economic, social and political life of our country and of our time, and that one among these concepts is the right of the workers to be heard through a representative and spokesman of their own.

SAMUEL GOMPERS

Walter Adams: THE STEEL INDUSTRY

BEFORE 1898, the steel industry was the scene of active and, at times, destructive competition. In this early period, various gentlemen's agreements and pools were organized in an effort to control the production of steel rails, billets, wire, nails and other products, but the outstanding characteristic of these agreements was the "frequency with which they collapsed."[1] Their weakness was that inherent in any pool or gentlemen's agreement, namely that "60 per cent of the agreers are gentlemen, 30 per cent just act like gentlemen, and 10 per cent neither are nor act like gentlemen." If production and prices were to be controlled, these loose-knit agreements had to be superseded by more stable forms of organization. The latter came upon the industry with a suddenness and intensity seldom paralleled in American industrial history.

From 1898 to 1900, a vast concentration movement took place in the steel industry. Large companies such as Federal Steel, National Steel, National Tube, American Bridge, and American Sheet Steel were organized. Dominated by three financial interest groups—Carnegie, Morgan, and Moore—these consolidations did not succeed in bringing "stability" to the industry. In fact, a fight between the newly formed giants seemed unavoidable.

Since each of the major interest groups was peculiarly vulnerable in case

a "battle between the giants" materialized, and since cooperation promised to be more profitable than competition, stubbornness yielded to reason. In 1901, with the initiative of Charles Schwab, J. P. Morgan, and a corporation lawyer named James B. Dill, the interested parties agreed to form the "combination of combinations"—the U.S. Steel Corporation which at the time of its formation controlled approximately 65 per cent of the nation's steel capacity. The size of the $62,500,000 promotion fee which accrued to the Morgan banking syndicate immediately aroused "the suspicion that here, as in earlier combinations, the security issue was greatly inflated."[2] Later investigation by the Commissioner of Corporations has justified this suspicion, for it was found that of the corporation's total capitalization of $1,402,846,817 only about half, $676,000,000, represented investment in tangible property. The rest, i.e., $726,846,817 minus reasonable allowance for good will, indicates, of course, the amount of excess capitalization or stock watering[3] which, over a period of years, was eventually squeezed out of the capital structure and replaced with tangible assets in the form of mills and mines.

Considerable disagreement has attended discussions of the motives behind

---

[1] H. R. Seager and C. A. Gulick, *Trust and Corporation Problems*, New York: Harper, 1929, p. 216. This book is an excellent source on the early history of U. S. Steel.

[2] *Ibid.*, p. 224.
[3] In his testimony before the Stanley Committee in 1911, Judge Moore defended such stock watering as not at all unusual. Said the judge: "Everybody knows what they [*sic!*] are getting when they get common stock. . . . They know they are not getting anything that represents assets."

the organization of the U.S. Steel Corporation. The announced motives were to form a completely integrated steel company; to secure the advantages of the most advanced technical organization; and to develop an extensive export trade. Judge Gary testified that the latter was the "dominating factor" favoring the creation of the corporation.[4] Most disinterested observers, however, agree that the "intent to monopolize" played a significant and perhaps dominant role. The policies of the corporation, subsequent to its organization in 1901, seem to bear out this opinion; for the corporation proceeded to acquire properties which would put it in a position to dominate the steel industry. Especially significant was the acquisition of essential raw material assets, particularly coking coal and iron ore mines.

By 1907, however, the corporation became concerned with more immediate problems than the long-run elimination of *potential* competition through a monopolization of some raw material supplies. It had to face a spasm of *active* price competition which had been brought on by the business panic of that year. To meet this challenge and to restore price stability under its own leadership, it innovated the famous Gary dinners. The purpose of these dinners— in the words of the host, the president of U.S. Steel—was "to maintain to a reasonable extent the equilibrium of business, to prevent utter demoralization of business and destructive competition."[5] Mr. Gary *achieved* this objective by urging "his guests, who represented fully 90 per cent of the industry, that they co-operate in holding prices where they were."[6] . . .

Available evidence indicates that the dinners were held at irregular intervals until 1911. However, when the government became increasingly suspicious of their price-fixing function and when it finally filed suit for the dissolution of U.S. Steel, the dinners were abruptly abandoned. But the damage had been done. The Corporation stood accused in the Federal courts as a monopoly, and the government demanded the extreme penalty—dissolution.

Due to the outbreak of World War I, the case was not decided until 1920 when the fervor of earlier trust-busting campaigns had died down. By a vote of 4 to 3, the Supreme Court decided against dissolution.[7] Without considering the effects of price quotation under the Pittsburgh-Plus system, the court declared that mere size was no offense. While conceding that U.S. Steel was guilty of an attempt to monopolize the steel industry, the court maintained that such a monopoly had never actually been achieved. However, if any one factor responsible for the court's rejection of the government plea were singled out, it would undoubtedly be the friendly attitude which U.S. Steel evidenced toward its competitors. This fact more than anything else probably explains why U.S. Steel was allowed to survive while the Standard Oil Company and the American Tobacco Company were unceremoniously dissolved. This was a vindication of a policy very close to Judge Gary's heart, a policy over which there was considerable dispute with the corporation's board of directors; for

---

[4] *Hearings before the House Committee on Investigation of the U.S. Steel Corporation,* Vol I, p. 104; hereafter referred to as *Stanley Hearings* (1911).
[5] *Stanley Hearings,* Vol. I, p. 264.

[6] Ida M. Tarbell, *The Life of Elbert H. Gary,* New York: Appleton, 1926, p. 205.
[7] *United States v. United States Steel Corp.,* 251 U.S. 417 (1920).

Gary's "Directors, worthy men but of a cruder age, were honestly puzzled. It was bewildering to hear their Chairman preach the community of interests of all steelmakers, to see him consistently refusing to use the Corporation's size as a club over the rest of the industry. Destructive competition, they pointed out, had made hundreds of millions for Rockefeller's oil trust. But the day came when Gary could point out that the oil trust was busted and that the steel trust had survived, and that its survival was largely due to his policy of 'friendly competition.' "[8]

After 1920, U.S. Steel continued to dominate the industry, although its percentage control over total industry sales declined steadily. The corporation remained sufficiently big, however, to keep its competitors "in line" without threats and without displays of force. The friendly competition, which had paid such handsome dividends in the past, endured as the basic characteristic of the industry....

---

[8] "U.S. Steel: I," reprinted from *Fortune*, Vol. XIII, March 1936, p. 157, by special permission of the Editors. Copyright Time, Inc.

Arundel Cotter: UNITED STATES STEEL—A CORPORATION WITH A SOUL

DURING the World War, there began to gather on the industrial horizon a cloud no bigger at first than a man's hand, but one that grew fast in size until it broke in a storm the effects of which made themselves felt in every corner of the globe.

This was a general feeling of unrest and dissatisfaction, by no means confined to one country or one class of people, but having its most virulent manifestations among the laboring classes, the proletariat. This unrest was fostered and seized upon by radical leaders everywhere to further their own ambitions, their object being the overthrow of capital, the nationalization of industry, and their own aggrandizement.

Nor were they without considerable success in some countries. Russia, of course, provided the most notable example, and England today is suffering by reason of the same forces; but the United States, notwithstanding its aloofness from the centre of disturbance, its prosperity, and the general high average of common sense among its inhabitants, did not entirely escape.

Here the radical manifestations took the form of industrial strikes which broke out sporadically in all quarters. It was natural that the steel industry should not be immune. In fact, it was inevitable that steel, more than any other industry, should be selected for especial attention by those who hoped to do away with private ownership and to establish mob rule.

Among the reasons that may be cited for the selection of the steel industry, and the United States Steel Corporation in particular, for a grand attack by the radical forces were the following:

Steel was "open shop." Since 1892, when the Carnegie Steel Co., in one of the bloodiest and bitterest industrial conflicts in history, crushed the Homestead strike, the labor leaders' unions had never succeeded in regaining a foothold in the trade, and it was looked upon as a lost province by labor leaders who never abandoned the hope of some day organizing the steel workers. This fact gave the radicals in the labor ranks confidence that they could count upon the support of the usually conservative heads of organized labor in America to further their plans if steel were chosen as a battleground. And the events proved that their confidence was not misplaced.

Further, the physical necessities of steel making are hard on the worker. Although employers have done much to ameliorate conditions in the mills and mines, it is impossible to make the work really pleasant and it was therefore comparatively easy to give verisimilitude to distorted statements regarding the hard lot of the steel worker.

Again, a large percentage of the common labor in the steel plants was of alien birth, usually lacking in education and easily influenced by inflammatory doctrines.

Labor leaders, doubtless, also believed that the long litigation which the Government had conducted against the Steel Corporation had turned public sentiment

From *United States Steel* by Arundel Cotter (Garden City, N.Y.: Doubleday, Page and Company, 1921), pp. 246–268.

against the big company. If this was a factor in their calculations they were sadly deceived.

So, briefly, we have the genesis of the steel strike—the determination of organized labor to absorb steel workers and the seizing upon this by the radicals as the tool to further their own anarchistic ends.

The strike, when it came, was inaugurated ostensibly to compel the manufacturers to grant recognition to union "representatives" of the workers. Steel company officials claimed that its real object was twofold—to force upon the industry the "closed shop," and to overthrow the social scheme upon which the American Republic was grounded.

Labor leaders throughout the struggle consistently denied any intention of forcing a closed shop. And it is true that they at no time demanded this in so many words; but the closed shop would have resulted inevitably had they won. One has only to examine their demands to realize this.

And the lust for power on the part of the leaders of organized labor was used by the radicals as a tool with which they hoped to gain a much greater goal than the closed shop—the nationalization of the steel industry and, using that as a wedge, of all American industry.

In fighting and smashing the strike the Steel Corporation performed an invaluable service, not alone to its stockholders or to capital, but to the vast majority of workers who claimed the right to work at their own volition and not the dictates of self-appointed leaders: a service to the American public at large.

Says Mr. Charles Piez, one-time head of the Emergency Fleet Corporation, in a recent article in *The Independent:*

The real or imaginary wrongs of the workers played not the slightest part in the decision to organize the steel industry.

It was a citadel of the open shop that was the subject of attack; it was the last barrier against complete and final unionization of American industry, against which Foster and Fitzpatrick combined their wits and resources.

And it is to the everlasting credit of Judge Gary that he successfully resisted this attack, for it is to the interests of the public that the principle of the open shop be sustained.

How important to the labor unions was the hope for organization of the Steel Corporation is obvious. Between 500,000 and 600,000 workers are engaged in the industry, the Corporation alone employing about 275,000. Possibly another half million are employed in closely allied industries. And the steel trade, as well as these allied industries, has for years looked to the Corporation for guidance on important questions of public polity. Hence, United States Steel's adherence to the open-shop principle was a deep and rankling wound in the side of the labor unions.

So long as the big enterprise of which Judge Gary is head remained outside of the union's fold there was small hope of herding into it any material number of workers in other plants. U.S. Steel was a citadel of the open shop, the bulwark between free and union labor. If it could be converted from "open" to "closed" shop, the early unionization, not of the steel trade merely, but of all American industry, would follow, and the power of the union leaders would be expanded to an almost illimitable extent.

It is doubtful if the older and wiser among the union chieftains would have forced the issue at the time they did had they been left to their own decisions. But they were not. They had the radical element to reckon with.

It is perhaps unnecessary to explain that organized labor in the United

States is divided into two parts: On the one hand, there is the American Federation of Labor, headed by Samuel Gompers, and including the great majority of unionized workers. This organization recognizes property rights and is loyal to the principles of American government. But its leaders, being only human, are apparently determined to bring all industry under its sway and are impatient of the ideas of those workers who prefer to stand on their own feet.

On the other hand, there is a smaller organization, the Industrial Workers of the World, better known as the I.W.W. or, sometimes, the "I Won't Works." "The wobblies," as they prefer to call themselves, are as bitterly opposed to the principles of the larger Federation as they are to capital. Chief among their tenets is the Marxian fallacy that labor produces all and capital nothing and that, therefore, capital must be abolished.

Some years ago there arose to prominence in the councils of the I.W.W. one William Z. Foster, a man of unquestioned ability but of principles dangerous and subversive to government. These principles he set forth in a book on "Syndicalism," a book which constitutes one of the most extreme examples of anarchistical literature. Foster characterizes the wage system as "the most brazen and gigantic robbery ever perpetrated since the world began."

Although advocating the most drastic measures for the overthrow of capital, Foster was apparently sufficiently astute to realize that a vast majority of the American people, and even of organized labor, would not and could not accept his views, and that the I.W.W. which did was not a powerful enough weapon with which to achieve his ends.

He believed, however, and events proved that he was not mistaken, that the American Federation of Labor could be inoculated with radicalism if the poison were spread from the inside. He therefore publicly advocated what he described as the process of "boring from within," urging that the radicals join the more conservative Federation and, once inside that body, disseminate their vicious doctrines from within.

Not long after this we find Foster a member of the Federation, ostensibly converted from his I.W.W. leanings, enjoying the confidence of Gompers and his co-workers, and high in their councils. His "boring" process had met with eminent success.

Meanwhile, the World War was approaching its end, leaving in its wake a world-wide wave of industrial unrest. Russia was being misgoverned by its most radical element, who held their power in the midst of a sea of blood. Communistic doctrines were being preached, openly or *sub rosa,* in every land and clime. American labor was restless, and the foreign element, particularly, showed that it had been infected with the fever of anarchism that was rampant in parts of Europe. The time had come for the radicals to strike, for the "boring-from-within" process to bear fruit. . . .

But while the labor leaders had been busy collecting dues from and enlisting sympathy for the "oppressed" steel workers there had, strange to say, come no call for help from the steel workers themselves. They made no claim of being downtrodden; rather did many of them resent, as a slur on their manhood, the insinuation that they were. The union chiefs have since claimed that they were appealed to by the workers, but not one iota of evidence has ever been adduced to support this claim. . . .

Their first move was the sending of a letter by Samuel Gompers to Judge Gary, asking the head of the Steel Corporation to meet a union deputation to discuss questions affecting the welfare of the workers. This letter was never answered. . . .

Whether it might not have been wiser had Judge Gary answered Mr. Gompers' letter and obviated the possibility of any misunderstanding by giving the correspondence to the press is an open question. But he was probably averse to being drawn into what would likely prove the beginning of a long epistolatory controversy with the head of the Labor Federation. This could not but have had an unsettling effect on the more easily influenced among the steel workers, playing into Gompers' hands.

It is also not unlikely that Judge Gary believed the labor unions were resolved on forcing the issue of organizing the steel industry and that any verbal preliminaries to the conflict would be worse than useless. . . .

. . . The steel companies generally have been trying for years to institute a real eight-hour day and have made the eight-hour day the basis of wage payments. Practically all steel workers work only six days a week. The twenty-four-hour shift is borne by a very small percentage of the workers and by these only on widely separated occasions. The Corporation and its competitors as well, following its lead, have repeatedly advanced wages without solicitation from the men, and the claim that the wage they pay is insufficient to permit American standards of living has not borne investigation.

But the acceptance of such demands as the recognition of the right of collective bargaining, coupled with the check-off system of collecting union dues and assessments, would have handed over the companies, bound hand and foot, to the unions. The application of the seniority principle in maintaining, reducing,

and increasing working forces would have obviously made for inefficiency and destroyed the incentive to effort and good work on the part of the men. Finally, physical examination of applicants for employment in an industry where sound health, active muscles, and keen eyesight are necessary not only for the safety of the worker himself, but for that of his associates, was a precaution which the companies could not dispense with in fairness either to themselves or to their employees. . . .

Nothing actually happened, however, until the 26th of that month. On that day a committee of union leaders composed of the five gentlemen whom Gompers had previously asked Judge Gary to meet arrived in New York City and called at the offices of the Corporation seeking an interview, only to meet with another polite refusal. . . .

Shortly before this the President of the United States had announced his intention of calling an "Industrial Conference" at Washington, beginning October 6th, to consider the grave industrial questions facing the country in the wake of the World War, and particularly the relations between capital and labor. It was obvious that one of the President's reasons for calling the conference at this time was to forestall the threatened steel strike, which had been brewing for months, and to bring about, if possible, harmonious relations between the steel companies and organized labor.

But the President did not stop there. He used the power of his great office in every legitimate way to ward off the blow that was threatening the country's industry. Bernard M. Baruch, former head of the War Industries Board, was commissioned by Mr. Wilson to endeavor to persuade Judge Gary to confer with the unions, but Mr. Baruch was unable to change the attitude of the head of the

Corporation, who saw plainly what few others realized at the time, that the issue was not merely that of a strike, but that the very foundations of the country's liberty were threatened, and that it was no time for compromising. On the 10th of September, when all hope of averting the strike seemed gone, the President made still another effort and dispatched a telegram to Samuel Gompers, urging that action be postponed until after the Industrial Conference.

At this time the situation stood thus: The organized portion of the steel trade had voted to strike, leaving details and the decision as to the date in the hands of the committee already named. Mr. Gompers referred the President's letter to the committee, which had full power to comply with the request of the nation's Chief Executive, but the committee declared that postponement was out of the question. The strike date was set for September 22nd, on which day, the union leaders confidently asserted, there would not be a wheel turning or fire burning in any steel mill west of the Alleghanies.

Thus was the fatal die cast. From that time both sides girded up their loins and prepared for the conflict.

The steel companies expressed quiet confidence in the outcome, while their opponents loudly boasted of certain victory. The officials of the Steel Corporation and of the other companies threatened must have known that a considerable element among their foreign-born employees had been led astray by the radical preachings of labor organizers, but they believed that the best element among their men was satisfied with conditions and would continue at work. And this confidence proved justified.

The steel trade, outside the Corporation, had been watching the issue with some misgiving, but as it became plain that Judge Gary was standing firm in his attitude, general satisfaction was evident and confidence in the final result increased. For the trade was not unduly worried as to the outcome in the event of a showdown. The opinion generally expressed was that the issue must be forced sooner or later, and that it was probably best to have it settled as speedily as possible by a decisive conflict. But in many quarters apprehension was felt that the Judge, realizing his immense responsibility, might allow himself to be persuaded into a compromise.

However, Judge Gary was firm, as those who knew him best were sure he would be. For there was a matter of principle involved, the right of the independent worker to work when, where, and with whom he desired and could obtain employment. And for Judge Gary, compromise on questions of principle was out of the question. As this became realized, all misgivings vanished. Judge Gary's already recognized position as leader of the steel industry was made more secure than ever before. The trade left the issue in his hands, assured as to the result, and this assurance was not abused.

It is not too much to say that the entire country waited with bated breath for the events of September 22nd. It was recognized that this was not a mere skirmish between employer and employee, but a gigantic struggle between capital and radical labor. As time wore on it developed that there was another and stronger party to the conflict, the vast mass of unorganized workers; and this threw its strength on the side of the Corporation, dooming the hopes of the strike leaders.

At first the strike organizers unquestionably struck hard and with considerable result. Between the conflicting claims from all sides it is impossible to say just how many men went out in the steel mills, voluntarily or through intimidation, but it is certain that at many centres, such as Youngstown, where the Corporation and some of the larger independents—Republic Iron & Steel, Youngstown Sheet & Tube and Brier Hill Steel—have big plants, operations were practically suspended in toto. At Gary, the Corporation's largest plant, operations were reduced to a low point, and at many other centres, the results, at the outset, were apparently in favor of the strikers.

But Pittsburgh, the world's steel centre, was almost unaffected. At Homestead, Braddock, Duquesne, and other big Corporation plants the workers unequivocally proved their loyalty by sticking to their jobs, and the strike leaders failed utterly to make headway. Day after day the smoke ascending in volumes from the stacks of these plants gave assurance that the steel companies were far from crippled and sent to the union chiefs the message of certain defeat unless they could succeed in quenching these furnaces.

Although, ostensibly, the strike was directed against the Steel Corporation and no attempt had been made to negotiate with the heads of other concerns, all steel companies west of the Alleghanies were affected by the walk-out as much as or more than was the Corporation. So far as the big company was concerned, the greatest number of men out when the strike was at its worst, or within a few days of its inception, was 28 per cent of its total of employees or 40 per cent of its manufacturing force. These were the figures given by Judge Gary in his testimony at Washington in October, and undoubtedly they are as nearly accurate as possible. And of the men out there is no question that many were kept from work not by persuasion but by intimidation, the strikers having used threats freely to keep the loyal workers from the mills.

Such tactics are not at all a new thing in similar conditions. Steel workers who sought to report for duty were sent letters threatening them with injury or death to themselves or families. In some cases the threats were sent to the men's wives or other dependents where their effect was perhaps greater.

The strike had not been in progress two days before its genesis became patent. The American public soon realized that probably 98 per cent of the strikers were alien-born and that the native worker, with few exceptions, and large numbers of naturalized foreigners, were sticking to the steel companies. This, together with the inflammatory utterances of the strikers themselves, convinced the public that the strike was not what it claimed to be, an effort to get fair wages and improved living conditions for the workers—the American workers who remained at their posts insisted that they already had these and the evidence adduced by the steel companies verified the statement—but an attempt to deliver the steel mills and factories into the hands of the radical foreign element among our industrial workers. It was, in a word, but the first step toward the seizure of the means of production by labor.

And the public, with the example of Russia before it, could not and did not sympathize with the strikers.

With some notable exceptions the strike was a bloodless one. This was due principally to the prompt action taken by the local public authorities at the various points affected to prevent trouble and to the refusal of the steel companies generally to attempt to bring in strike breakers. Because of this passive attitude on the part of the employers the strikers were robbed of the opportunity to make sufficient trouble to force intervention by the Government.

In no previous conflict between capital and labor, it is likely, has the public had as excellent an opportunity of judging the rights and wrongs as in the steel strike. One day after the struggle eventually began the Senate of the United States passed a resolution instructing the Committee on Education and Labor to investigate the strike and report on its causes. The committee conducted public hearings in Washington where Judge Gary and a number of loyal workers were heard on the side of the Steel Corporation, while Foster, Fitzpatrick, Gompers, and other union leaders had equal opportunity, which they availed themselves of, to present their case. The committee also visited the affected districts to secure first-hand evidence on conditions there.

In an essentially fair and complete report, submitted to the Senate on November 8, 1919, the committee reviewed the claims of the strike leaders and of the Corporation. While criticizing the steel companies on the question of too long work hours and suggesting that the six-day week could be extended to include all workers, the report characterized some of the statements of the strike organizers as false and dismissed their claim of pauper wages, expressing the opinion that the employees of the steel industry were fairly well satisfied with wages received and that the question of wages was not persuasive at all in the consideration of a strike. The committee, in fact, in its own language found little to complain of as to conditions in general outside of long work hours.

On the other hand, the committee reported the underlying cause of the strike to be "the determination of the American Federation of Labor to organize the steel workers in opposition to the known and long-established policy of the industry against organization," and the "seizing upon this cause by some radicals who are seeking to elevate themselves to power in the A.F. of L."

On this point the committee further found that "behind this strike there is massed a considerable element of I.W.W.'s, anarchists, revolutionists, and Russian soviets," and expressed the opinion that the American Federation of Labor had "made a serious mistake by permitting the leadership of this strike movement to pass into the hands of some who have entertained most radical and dangerous doctrines."

Still further pursuing this point the committee reported: "There may be, in view of the radical utterances and actions of certain strike leaders, some warrant for the belief that the strike in the steel industry is a part of a general scheme and purpose on the part of radical leaders to bring about a general industrial revolution. The committee, however, do not go to that extent because they feel there were some real grievances." This, of course, is just what steel men and the greater part of the public believe.

While this report served to prove that the conclusions arrived at long before by the great mass of the public were correct, the strike was dying out before it was presented. In fact, the majority of the steel mills of the country had resumed nearly full operations by early in November. The strike gradually lessened in importance from the end of September and, although it was not actually called off by its leaders until nearly the middle of January it was to all practical purposes dead long before the end of the year.

The story of the Industrial Conference

called by President Wilson in an effort to bring together the conflicting forces of capital and organized labor and to work out a new industrial scheme rightly belongs with that of the steel strike. . . .

. . . The labor leaders undoubtedly, by the time the Conference came together on October 6th, realized that in their conflict with the Steel Corporation and the steel companies generally they had engaged in a losing fight. At the very time strikers in large numbers were going back to the mills and the operations of the steel companies were steadily increasing. The continuation of the fight meant a total loss to the unions while arbitration would have permitted them to gain some of their points, or at least to yield gracefully and save their faces. They saw, or thought they saw, in the Industrial Conference, a means to force the Corporation to accept arbitration. . . .

As it proved, the method adopted by Judge Gary in fighting the strike was the best. It consisted principally of permitting the public every opportunity of judging all aspects of the case and of standing pat on the fairness of the steel companies in dealing with their men. Had the Judge yielded one iota to the demands of the labor organizers this would but have convinced the radical element in labor that they held the whip hand over capital and would have encouraged them to further excessive demands. Had the Judge, on the other hand, attempted to fight the strike by meeting violence with violence this would have alienated public sympathy. And in the final analysis public opinion is the most important factor in settling industrial disputes.

As an aftermath to the strike came the "investigation" by the Interchurch World Movement, an organization at the head of which were a number of bishops and other churchmen. A Committee of this organization visited Pittsburgh and other points and presented a statement, but it was of a character entirely biased against the Corporation, its members, in their investigation, having apparently given heed only to the arguments of Messrs. Foster and Fitzpatrick.

In the report of this committee stress is laid on the long working hours of the man in the steel mill, ignoring the fact that steel companies generally have made great effort to reduce the average of daily work and that only a comparatively small percentage of the men work twelve hours. Further, the committee attacked the Corporation on the question of wages which it declared to be below the sum required for American standards of living, its statements failing to harmonize with the findings of other obviously unprejudiced investigators including the Senate Committee on Education and Labor, which found otherwise.

In standing on a just basis and refusing to follow the easier way of compromise the Steel Corporation performed a service not to itself or to the steel trade alone. It performed a service to the whole country and even to the world. It gave the first decided check to the growing strength of radicalism which was then threatening to overwhelm America and prevented a situation which would have thrown the country into the same condition that has for some time prevailed in Russia.

The evil of unchecked growth of unionism is illustrated by what is happening in England at the present writing. The Corporation saved this country from similar evils. By its stand it established the right of every worker to earn a livelihood whether or not he belongs to a union.

William Z. Foster: THE GREAT STEEL STRIKE AND ITS LESSONS

THE great steel strike lasted three months and a half. Begun on September 22, 1919, by 365,000 men quitting their places in the iron and steel mills and blast furnaces in fifty cities of ten states, it ended on January 8, 1920, when the organizations affiliated in the National Committee for Organizing Iron and Steel Workers voted to permit the 100,000 or more men still on strike to return to work upon the best terms they could secure.

The steel manufacturers "won" the strike. By forcing an unconditional surrender, they drove their men back to the old slavery. This they accomplished in their wonted and time-honored way by carrying on a reign of terror that outraged every just conception of civil and human rights. In this unholy task they were aided by a crawling, subservient and lying press, which spewed forth its poison propaganda in their behalf; by selfish and indifferent local church movements, which had long since lost their Christian principles in an ignominious scramble for company favors; and by hordes of unscrupulous municipal, county, state and federal officials, whose eagerness to wear the steel collar was equalled only by their forgetfulness of their oaths of office. No suppression of free speech and free assembly, no wholesale clubbing, shooting and jailing of strikers and their families was too revolting for these Steel Trust[1] hangers-on to carry out with

relish. With the notable exception of a few honorable and courageous individuals here and there among these hostile elements, it was an alignment of the steel companies, the state, the courts, the local churches and the press against the steel workers.

Upon the ending of the strike the steel workers got no direct concessions from their employers. Those who were able to evade the bitter blacklist were compelled to surrender their union cards and to return to work under conditions that are a shame and a disgrace. They were driven back to the infamous peonage system with its twelve hour day, a system which American steel workers, of all those in the world, alone have to endure. In England, France, Italy and Germany, the steel workers enjoy the right of a voice in the control of their industry; they regularly barter and bargain with their employers over the questions of hours, wages and working conditions; they also have the eight hour day. One must come to America, the land of freedom, to find steel workers still economically disfranchised and compelled to work

[1] Throughout this book the term "Steel Trust" is used to indicate the collectivity of the great steel companies. It is true that this is in contradiction to the common usage, which generally applies the term to the United States Steel Corporation alone, but it is in harmony with the facts. All the big steel companies act together upon all important matters confronting their industry. Beyond question they are organized more or less secretly into a trust. This book recognizes this situation, hence the broad use of the term "Steel Trust." It is important to remember this explanation. Where the writer has in mind any one company that company is named.

From *The Great Steel Strike and Its Lessons* by William Z. Foster, pp. 1–4, 8–10, 13–19, 21, 23–30, 32–35, 37, 40–49, 68–69, 74–88, 90–91, 93–94, 96–97, 99–101, 105–106, 109. Copyright 1920, by B. W. Heubsch, Inc., New York. Reprinted by permission of The Viking Press, Inc.

twelve hours a day. In this country alone the human rights of the steel workers are crushed under foot by the triumphant property rights of their employers. . . .

There are a hundred good reasons why the principles of collective bargaining and the shorter workday should prevail in the steel industry of America, and only one why they should not. This one reason is that the industry is hard and fast in the grip of absentee capitalists who take no part in production and whose sole function is to seize by hook or crook the product of the industry and consume it. These parasites, in their voracious quest of profits, know neither pity nor responsibility. Their reckless motto is "After us the deluge." . . .

The recent upheaval in the steel industry was but one link in a long chain of struggles, the latest battle in an industrial war for freedom which has raged almost since the inception of the industry. . . .

Against this will-to-power of their employers the steel workers have fought long and valiantly. In the early days of the industry, when the combinations of capital were weak, the working force skilled, English-speaking and independent, the latter easily defended themselves and made substantial progress toward their own inevitable, even if unrecognized goal of industrial freedom; but in later years, with the growth of the gigantic United States Steel Corporation, the displacement of skilled labor by automatic machinery and the introduction of multitudes of illiterate immigrants into the industry, their fight for their rights became a desperate and almost hopeless struggle. For the past thirty years they have suffered an unbroken series of defeats. Their one-time growing freedom has been crushed. . . .

At the outbreak of the World War the steel workers generally, with the exception of the laborers, who had secured a cent or two advance per hour, were making less wages than before the Homestead strike. The constant increase in the cost of living in the intervening years had still further depressed their standards of life. Not a shred of benefit had they received from the tremendously increased output of the industry. While the employers lived in gorgeous palaces, the workers found themselves, for the most part, crowded like cattle into the filthy hovels that ordinarily constitute the greater part of the steel towns. Tuberculosis ran riot among them; infant mortality was far above normal. Though several increases in wages were granted after the war began, these have been offset by the terrific rise in the cost of living. If the war has brought any betterment in the living conditions of the steel workers, it cannot be seen with the naked eye.

The twelve hour day prevails for half of the men. One-fourth work seven days a week, with a twenty-four hour shift every two weeks. Their lives are one constant round of toil. They have no family life, no opportunity for education or even for recreation; for their few hours of liberty are spoiled by the ever-present fatigue. Furthermore, working conditions in the mills are bad. The men are speeded up to such a degree that only the youngest and strongest can stand it. At forty the average steel worker is played out. The work, in itself extremely dangerous, is made still more so by the employers' failure to adopt the necessary safety devices. Many a man has gone to his death through the wanton neglect of the companies to provide safeguarding appliances that they would have been compelled to install were the unions still in the plants.[2] Not a trace of industrial

[2] The practice of the different steel companies varies with respect to safety devices. Some of them are still in the dark ages that all were in

justice remains. The treatment of the men depends altogether upon the arbitrary wills of the foremen and superintendents. A man may give faithful service in a plant for thirty years and then be discharged offhand, as many are, for some insignificant cause. He has not one to appeal to. His fellow workers, living in constant terror of discharge and the blacklist, dare not even listen to him, much less defend his cause. He must bow to the inevitable, even though it means industrial ruin for him and his family. . . .

From just previous to, until some time after the beginning of the World War the situation in the steel industry, from a trade-union point of view, was truly discouraging. It seemed impossible for the workers to accomplish anything by organized effort. . . .

But as the war wore on and the United States joined the general slaughter, the situation changed rapidly in favor of the unions. . . . It was an opportunity to organize the industry such as might never again occur. That the trade union movement did not embrace it sooner was a calamity.

The writer was one of those who perceived the unparalleled opportunity. But being at that time Secretary-Treasurer of the committee organizing the packing industry I was unable to do anything substantial in the steel situation until the handing down of Judge Alschuler's decision giving the packing house workers the eight hour day and other vital con-

cessions enabled me to slacken my efforts in that important movement. Immediately thereafter, on April 7, 1918, I presented a resolution to the Chicago Federation of Labor requesting the executive officers of the American Federation of Labor to call a general labor conference and to inaugurate thereat a national campaign to organize the steel workers. The resolution was endorsed by twelve local unions in the steel industry. It was adopted unanimously and forwarded to the A.F. of L. The latter took the matter up with the rapidly reviving Amalgamated Association, and the affair was slowly winding along to an eventual conference, with a loss of much precious time, when the resolution was re-submitted to the Chicago Federation of Labor, re-adopted and sent to the St. Paul convention of the A.F. of L., June 10–20, 1918. . . .

The resolution was adopted by unanimous vote. Accordingly, a number of conferences were held during the convention, at which the proposed campaign was discussed and endorsed. The outcome was that provisions were made to have President Gompers call another conference, in Chicago thirty days later, of responsible union officials who would come prepared to act in the name of their international unions. This involved further waste of probably the most precious time for organizing work that Labor will ever have. . . . The idea was to make a hurricane drive simultaneously in all the steel centers that would catch the workers' imagination and sweep them into the unions *en masse* despite all opposition, and thus to put Mr. Gary and his associates into such a predicament that they would have to grant the just demands of their men. . . . The fateful conference met in the New Morrison Hotel, Chicago, August 1–2, 1918. Sam-

---

a few years ago, with reckless disregard of human life. Others have made some progress. Of these the U.S. Steel Corporation is undoubtedly in the lead, for it has installed many safety appliances and has safety committees actively at work. At best, however, steel making is an exceedingly dangerous industry and the risk is intensified by the great heat of the mills and the long hours of work—the twelve hour day and the seven day week—which lead inevitably to exhaustion.

uel Gompers presided over its sessions. Representatives of fifteen international unions were present. . . .

At the same meeting the National Committee for Organizing Iron and Steel Workers was formed. It was made to consist of one representative from each of the cooperating international unions. Its given function was to superintend the work of organization. Its chairman had to be a representative of the A.F. of L. Mr. Gompers volunteered to fill this position; the writer was elected Secretary-Treasurer. Including later additions, the constituent unions were as follows:

International Brotherhood of Blacksmiths, Drop-Forgers and Helpers
Brotherhood of Boilermakers and Iron Ship Builders and Helpers of America
United Brick and Clay Workers
Bricklayers', Masons' and Plasterers' International Union of America
International Association of Bridge, Structural and Ornamental Iron Workers
Coopers' International Union of North America
International Brotherhood of Electrical Workers
International Brotherhood of Foundry Employees
International Hod Carriers', Building, and Common Laborers' Union of America
Amalgamated Association of Iron, Steel and Tin Workers
International Association of Machinists
International Union of Mine, Mill and Smelter Workers
United Mine Workers of America
International Molders' Union of North America
Patternmakers' League of North America
United Association of Plumbers and Steam Fitters
Quarry Workers' International Union of North America
Brotherhood Railway Carmen of America
International Seamen's Union of America
Amalgamated Sheet Metal Workers' International Alliance
International Brotherhood of Stationary Firemen and Oilers
International Union of Steam and Operating Engineers
International Brotherhood of Steamshovel and Dredgemen
Switchmen's Union of North America

This group of unions, lined up to do battle with the Steel Trust, represents the largest body of workers ever engaged in a joint movement in any country. Their members number approximately 2,000,000. . . .

The conference had removed the barriers in the way of the campaign. But when it came to providing the large sums of money and the numerous crews of organizers that were immediately and imperatively needed to insure success, it failed dismally. . . .

The slender resources in hand at once made necessary a complete change of strategy. To undertake a national movement was out of the question. The work had to be confined to the Chicago district. . . .

During the first week of September the drive for members was opened in the Chicago district. . . .

The inevitable happened; eager for a chance to right their wrongs, the steel workers stormed into the unions. . . . And it could just as well have been on a national scale, had the international unions possessed sufficient self-confidence and given enough men and money to put the original plan into execution. . . .

But now the folly of a one-district movement made itself evident. . . . The employers, applying Mr. Gary's famous "Give them an extra cup of rice" policy, ordered the basic eight hour day to go into effect on the first of October. This meant that the steel workers were to get thereafter time and one half after eight hours, instead of straight time. It amounted to an increase of two hours pay per day but the actual working hours were not changed. It was a counter stroke which the national movement had been designed to forestall. . . .

. . . Had the work been going on everywhere when Mr. Gary attempted this move, the workers would have understood his motives and joined the unions *en masse,*—the unions would have won hands down. . . .

Pittsburgh is the heart of America's steel industry. . . .

It was into this industrial labyrinth, the den of the Steel Trust, that the National Committee for Organizing Iron and Steel Workers moved its office on October 1, 1918, preparatory to beginning its work. . . .

The outlook was most unpromising. . . . Unfavorable winter weather was approaching. This was complicated by the influenza epidemic, which for several weeks suspended all public gatherings. Then came the end of the war. The workers had also just been given the basic eight hour day. . . . What was left of this interest was almost entirely wiped out when the mills, dependent as they were on war work, began to slacken production. The workers became obsessed with a fear of hard times, a timidity which was intensified by the steel companies' discharging every one suspected of union affiliations or sympathies. And to cap the climax, the resources of the National Committee were still pitifully inadequate to the great task confronting it.

But worst of all, the steel companies were now on the *Qui vive.* . . .

. . . In Pennsylvania, not to speak of other states, the workers enjoy few or no more rights than prevailed under the czars. They cannot hold meetings at all. So far are they below the status of prewar Germans in this respect that the comparative freedom of the latter seems almost like an unattainable idea. And this deprival of rights is done in the name of law and patriotism.

In the face of such suppression of constitutional rights and in the face of all the other staggering difficulties it was clearly impossible for our scanty forces to capture Pittsburgh for unionism by a frontal attack. Therefore a system of flank attacks was decided upon. This resolved itself into a plan literally to surround the immediate Pittsburgh district with organized posts before attacking it. . . .

Much of the success in these localities was due to the thoroughly systematic way in which the organizing work was carried on. This merits a brief description. There were two classes of organizers in the campaign, the floating and the stationary. Outside of a few traveling foreign speakers, the floating organizers were those sent in by the various international unions. They usually went about from point to point attending to their respective sections of the newly formed local unions, and giving such assistance to the general campaign as their other duties permitted. The stationary organizers consisted of A.F. of L. men, representatives of the United Mine Workers, and men hired directly by the National Committee. They acted as local organizing secretaries, and were the backbone of the working force. The floating organizers were controlled mostly by their international unions; the stationary organizers worked wholly under the direction of the National Committee.

Everywhere the organizing system used was the same. The local secretary was in full charge. He had an office, which served as general headquarters. He circulated the National Committee's weekly bulletin, consisting of a short, trenchant trade-union argument in four languages. He built up the mass meetings, and controlled all applications for membership. At these mass meetings and in the offices all trades were signed up indiscriminately upon a uniform blank. But there was no "one big union" formed. The signed applications were merely stacked away until there was a considerable number. Then the representatives of all the trades were assembled and the applications distributed among them. Later these men set up their respective unions. Finally, the new unions were drawn up locally into informal central bodies, known as Iron and Steel Workers' councils. These were invaluable as they knit the movement together and strengthened the weaker unions. They also inculcated the indispensable conception of solidarity along industrial lines and prevented irresponsible strike action by over-zealous single trades.

A highly important feature was the financial system. The handling of the funds is always a danger point in all working class movements. More than one strike and organizing campaign has been wrecked by loose money methods. The National Committee spared no pains to avoid this menace. The problem was an immense one, for there were from 100 to 125 organizers (which was what the crew finally amounted to) signing up steel workers by the thousands all over the country; but it was solved by the strict application of a few business principles. . . .

Practical labor officials who have handled mass movements understand the great difficulties attendant upon the organization of large bodies of workingmen. In the steel campaign these were more serious than ever before. The tremendous number of men involved; their unfamiliarity with the English language and total lack of union experience; the wide scope of the operations; the complications created by a score of international unions, each with its own corps of organizers, directed mainly from far-distant headquarters; the chronic lack of resources; and the need for quick action in the face of incessant attacks from the Steel Trust—all together produced technical difficulties without precedent. But the foregoing systems went far to solve them. And into these systems the organizers and secretaries entered wholeheartedly. They realized that modern labor organizations cannot depend wholly upon idealism. They bore in mind that they were dealing with human beings and had to adopt sound principles of responsibility, standardization and general efficiency.

. . . With hardly an exception, when the organizers went into a steel town to begin work they would be met by the local union men and solemnly assured that it was utterly impossible to organize the steel mills in their town. "But," the organizers would say, "we succeeded in organizing Gary and South Chicago and many other tough places." "Yes, we know that," would be the reply, "but conditions are altogether different here. These mills are absolutely impossible. We have worked on them for years and cannot make the slightest impression. They are full of scabs from all over the country. You will only waste your time by monkeying with them." This happened not in one place alone, but practically everywhere —illustrating the villainous reputation the steel companies had built up as union smashers.

Side-stepping these pessimistic croakers, the organizers would go on to their task with undiminished self-confidence and energy. The result was success everywhere. The National Committee can boast the proud record of never having set up its organizing machinery in a steel town without ultimately putting substantial unions among the employees. . . .

Each town produced its own particular crop of problems. . . . A few details about the work in Johnstown will suffice to indicate the tactics of the employers and the nature of the campaign generally.

Johnstown is situated on the main line of the Pennsylvania railroad, seventy-five miles east of Pittsburgh. It is the home of the Cambria Steel Company, which employs normally from 15,000 to 17,000 men in its enormous mills and mines. It is one of the most important steel centers in America.

For sixty-six years the Cambria Company had reared its black stacks in the Conemaugh valley and ruled as autocratically as any mediaeval baron. It practically owned the district and the dwellers therein. It paid its workers less than almost any other steel company in Pennsylvania and was noted as one of the country's worst union-hating concerns. . . .

Into this industrial jail of a city the National Committee went in the early winter of 1918–19, at the invitation of local steel workers who had heard of the campaign. . . . Immediately a strong organization spirit manifested itself—the wrongs of two-thirds of a century would out. It was interesting to watch the counter-moves of the company. They were typical. At first the officials contented themselves by stationing numbers of bosses and company detectives in front of the office and meeting halls to jot down the names of the men attending. But when this availed nothing, they took the next step by calling the live union spirits to the office and threatening them with dismissal. This likewise failed to stem the tide of unionism, and then the

company officials applied their most dreaded weapon, the power of discharge. . . .

Never was a policy of industrial frightfulness more diabolically conceived or more rigorously executed than that of the Cambria Steel Company. The men sacrificed were the Company's oldest and best employees. Men who had worked faithfully for ten, twenty or thirty years were discharged at a moment's notice. The plan was to pick out the men economically most helpless; men who were old and crippled, or who had large families dependent upon them, or homes half paid for, and make examples of them to frighten the rest. . . .

For months the Company continued these tactics.[3] Hundreds of union men were thus victimized. . . . But the terrorists overshot the mark. Human nature could not endure it. They goaded their workers to desperation and forced them to fight back, however unfavorable the circumstances. The National Committee met in Johnstown and ordered a ballot among the men. They voted overwhelmingly to strike. . . .

Company unions are invariably contemptible. All of them are cursed with company dictation, and all of them lack the vivifying principles of democratic control; but it is doubtful if a more degraded specimen can be found anywhere than that of the Cambria Steel Company. Without a murmur of protest it watched the company abolish the basic eight hour

[3] In its war against unionism the Cambria Steel Company held nothing sacred, not even the church. During the campaign the Reverend George Dono Brooks, pastor of the First Baptist Church of Johnstown, took an active part, speaking at many meetings and generally lending encouragement to the workers. For this crime the company punished him by disrupting his congregation and eventually driving him from the city, penniless.

day late in 1918. Nor did it raise a finger to help the multitude of unfairly discharged union men. It habitually pigeon-holed all real grievances submitted to it. But what else could be expected of a committee from which the company boldly discharged every man who dared say a word for the workers? . . .

. . . At all times a strike in Johnstown alone against the united steel companies was considered a move of desperation, a last resort to be undertaken only because nothing else could be done. But now relief was in sight. Spring was at hand and the national movement fast coming to a head. . . .

. . . In spite of the bitterest hardships they built up and developed their organizations. In this they were unwittingly but powerfully aided by the company union. Several weeks before the big strike the officials took the hated general committee to Atlantic City, wined them and dined them and flattered them, as usual, and then had them adopt a set of resolutions condemning the national movement of the steel workers and endorsing long hours, low wages and heavier production as the remedy for prevailing bad conditions. This betrayal was the last straw. It provoked intense resentment among the men. Whole battalions of them, the most skilled and difficult in the plant to organize, walked down and joined the unions in protest. Almost 3000 enrolled the week after the resolutions were adopted. But it was always thus. Every move that the Cambria made, the unions turned to their advantage. They outgeneraled the Company at every turn. . . .

. . . When the great strike broke on September 22 the Johnstown workers went into the fight almost one hundred per cent organized and with about the same percentage of grievances. . . . All the power of the great corporation, which had made $30,000,000 the year before, could not forestall the unions. It had no arrow in its quiver that could strike fear to the hearts of its workers; no trick in its brain pan that could be substituted for industrial democracy.

And Johnstown was only one point in the long battle line. Its experiences were but typical. . . .

Surging forward to the accomplishment of the "impossible," the organization of the steel industry, the twenty-four cooperating international unions found themselves in grips with the employers long before they were strong enough to sustain such a contest. . . . Following in the wake of the newly formed steel workers' unions came a mass of such difficulties requiring immediate settlement. The demand for relief from the evils of long hours, low wages and miserable working conditions was bad enough; but infinitely more serious was the need to take care of the army of men discharged for union membership. . . .

So bad was the situation by early spring that, lacking other means of relief, local strikes were threatening all over the country. . . . Therefore, the National Committee for Organizing Iron and Steel Workers called a general conference of delegates of steel workers' unions of all trades through the entire industry, to take place in Pittsburgh, May 25, 1919. The object was to demonstrate to the rank and file how fast the national movement was developing, to turn their attention to it strongly, and thus hearten them to bear their hardships until it could come to their assistance. . . . .

As the first approach, Mr. Gompers addressed the following letter to Mr. Gary, requesting a conference:

American Federation of Labor

The Alamac Hotel
Atlantic City, N.J.
June 20, 1919

Mr. Elbert H. Gary, Chairman,
Board of Directors, U.S. Steel Corporation,
New York, N.Y.

Dear Sir:

Of course you are aware that upon the request of a number of men in the employ of the United States Steel Corporation, and realizing the need of it, the convention of the American Federation of Labor decided to respond and give such assistance as is possible in order to bring about more thorough organization of the workers in the iron and steel industry, particularly those employed by your Corporation.

A campaign of organization was begun in June, 1918, and within that period we have secured the organization of more than 100,000 of the employees in the iron and steel industry. The prospects for the complete organization are, I am informed, exceedingly bright.

Of course, knowing the policy of the Organized Labor movement I have the honor in part to represent, we aim to accomplish the purposes of our labor movement; that is, better conditions for the toilers, by American methods, and American understandings, not by revolutionary methods or the inauguration of a cataclysm.

We believe in the effort of employer and employees to sit down around a table and, meeting thus, face to face, and having a better understanding of each other's position in regard to conditions of labor, to hours, standards, etc., and after reaching an amicable understanding to enter into an agreement for collective bargaining that is to cover wages, hours of labor, conditions of employment, etc.

At the Atlantic City convention of the American Federation of Labor just closed, the committee reported upon the progress made, and I am instructed and authorized to suggest to you whether you will consent to hold a conference with a committee representing not only the iron and steel workers who are organized, but representing the best interests of the unorganized men in the employ of your Corporation. The names of the committee I am asking you to meet are:

Assistant President Davis, Amalgamated Iron and Steel and Tin Workers.

William Hannon, member executive board, International Association of Machinists.

Edward Evans, representing International Brotherhood of Electrical Workers.

Wm. Z. Foster, secretary of the National Committee for Organizing Iron and Steel Workers and representing the Brotherhood of Carmen of America.

John Fitzpatrick, president Chicago Federation of Labor.

If you can advise me at your early convenience that the request contained in this letter meets with your approval and that a conference can be held, I am sure I shall be additionally appreciative.

Kindly address your reply, which I trust may be favorable, to the American Federation of Labor Building, Washington, D.C.

Respectfully yours,
SAMUEL GOMPERS
President, American
Federation of Labor

To Mr. Gompers' courteous letter Czar Gary did not deign to reply. This was bad. It looked like war. . . . Therefore, after waiting several weeks for word from Mr. Gary, the National Committee met, gave the situation profound consideration, and adopted the following resolution:

Resolution

WHEREAS, Working conditions in the steel industry are so intolerable and the unrest arising therefrom so intense that they can only be remedied by the application of the principles of collective bargaining; and,

WHEREAS, All efforts have failed to bring about a conference between the heads of the great steel corporations and the trade unions, representing many thousands of organized steel workers, for the purpose of establishing trade union conditions in the steel industry; therefore be it

RESOLVED, That the National Committee for Organizing Iron and Steel Workers recommends to its 24 affiliated unions that they take a strike vote of their local unions throughout the steel industry; and be it further

RESOLVED, That a special meeting be held in the Pittsburgh Labor Temple, July 20th, at 10 A.M. of representatives of all the cooperating international unions for the purpose of taking action on this matter.

. . . The resolution to take a strike vote of the men was re-adopted. Also the following general demands, based on accurate surveys of the situation, and subject to revision over the conference table, were formulated:

1. Right of collective bargaining
2. Reinstatement of all men discharged for union activities with pay for time lost
3. Eight-hour day
4. One day's rest in seven
5. Abolition of 24-hour shift
6. Increases in wages sufficient to guarantee American standard of living
7. Standard scales of wages in all trades and classifications of workers
8. Double rates of pay for all overtime after 8 hours, holiday and Sunday work
9. Check-off system of collecting union dues and assessments
10. Principles of seniority to apply in the maintenance, reduction and increase of working forces
11. Abolition of company unions
12. Abolition of physical examination of applicants for employment.

So plain, fair and equitable are these demands that to reasonable people they require no defense. The only explanation they might need relates to #9 and #12. The check-off was to apply only to the mining end of the steel industry, and the abolition of the physical examination

was to put a stop to the rank discrimination practiced by the companies through their medical departments. . . .

. . . Enthusiasm was intense. The steel workers saw a glimmer of hope and welcomed with open arms the opportunity to right their crying wrongs. . . .

. . . The vote was calculated conservatively at 98 per cent for a strike. The Conference Committee was accordingly instructed to request a conference with the heads of the United States Steel Corporation and the big independent companies, and if at the end of ten days no such meeting had been arranged, to set the strike date. . . .

Taking no further chances on unanswered letters, the Committee bearded Mr. Gary in his lair at 71 Broadway. He was in but refused to meet the Committee, requesting that its proposition be submitted in writing. The Committee thereupon sent him the following request for a conference:

New York, August 26, 1919

Hon. Elbert H. Gary,
Chairman Finance Committee
United States Steel Corporation
71 Broadway, New York City

Dear Sir:

During a general campaign of organization and education conducted under the auspices of the American Federation of Labor, many thousands of men employed in the iron and steel industry made application and were enrolled as members of the various organizations to which they were assigned.

This work has been carried on to a point where we feel justified in stating to you that we represent the sentiment of the vast majority of the employees in this industry, and acting on behalf of them, we solicit of you that a hearing be given to the undersigned Committee, who have been selected by the duly accredited representatives of the employees, to place before you matters that are of vital concern to them, and concerning

hours of labor, wages, working conditions
and the right of collective bargaining.

The Committee called at your office at
3 P.M., Tuesday, August 26, and requested
a conference. We were advised by your mes-
senger that you wished to be excused from a
personal interview at this time and requested
us to have our business in writing and whatever matters we wished to submit would be
taken up by yourself and your colleagues
and given consideration.

Therefore we are submitting in brief the
principal subjects that we desired to have a
conference on. The committee has an important meeting in another city on Thursday
next and will leave New York at 5 o'clock on
August 27, 1919. May we respectfully request that your answer be sent before that
time to Mr. John Fitzpatrick, Continental
Hotel, Broadway and Forty-first Street, New
York City.

> Very truly yours,
> JOHN FITZPATRICK
> D. J. DAVIS
> WM. HANNON
> EDW. J. EVANS
> WM. Z. FOSTER
> Committee

To this letter Mr. Gary replied as follows:

United States Steel Corporation
Office of the Chairman
New York, August 27, 1919
Messrs. John Fitzpatrick, David J. Davis,
William Hannon, Wm. Z. Foster, Edw. J.
Evans, Committee

Gentlemen:

Receipt of your communication of August
26 instant is acknowledged.

We do not think you are authorized to
represent the sentiment of a majority of the
employees of the United States Steel Corporation and its subsidiaries. We express no
opinion concerning any other members of
the iron and steel industry.

As heretofore publicly stated and repeated, our Corporation and subsidiaries,
although they do not combat labor unions

as such, decline to discuss business with
them. The Corporation and subsidiaries are
opposed to the "closed shop." They stand
for the "open shop," which permits one to
engage in any line of employment whether
one does or does not belong to a labor union. This best promotes the welfare of both
employees and employers. In view of the
well-known attitude as above expressed, the
officers of the Corporation respectfully decline to discuss with you, as representatives
of a labor union, any matter relating to employees. In doing so no personal discourtesy
is intended.

In all decisions and acts of the Corporation and subsidiaries pertaining to employees and employment their interests are of
highest importance. In wage rates, living and
working conditions, conservation of life and
health, care and comfort in times of sickness
or old age, and providing facilities for the
general welfare and happiness of employees
and their families, the Corporation and subsidiaries have endeavored to occupy a leading and advanced position among employers.

It will be the object of the Corporation
and subsidiaries to give such consideration
to employees as to show them their loyal
and efficient service in the past is appreci-
ated, and that they may expect in the future fair treatment.

> Respectfully yours,
> E. H. GARY, *Chairman*

In a last effort to prevail upon Mr.
Gary to yield his tyrannical position, the
committee addressed him this further
communication:

> New York City, Aug. 27, 1919
Hon. Elbert H. Gary, Chairman
Finance Committee,
United States Steel Corporation
71 Broadway, New York, N.Y.

Dear Sir:

We have received your answer to our request for a conference on behalf of the employees of your Corporation, and we understand the first paragraph of your answer to

be an absolute refusal on the part of your corporation to concede to your employees the right of collective bargaining.

You question the authority of our committee to represent the majority of your employees. The only way by which we can prove our authority is to put the strike vote into effect and we sincerely hope that you will not force a strike to prove this point.

We asked for a conference for the purpose of arranging a meeting where the questions of wages, hours, conditions of employment, and collective bargaining might be discussed. Your answer is a flat refusal for such conference, which raises the question, if the accredited representatives of your employees and the international unions affiliated with the American Federation of Labor and the Federation itself are denied a conference, what chance have the employees as such to secure any consideration of the views they entertain or the complaints they are justified in making.

We noted particularly your definition of the attitude of your Corporation on the question of the open and closed shop, and the positive declaration in refusing to meet representatives of union labor. These subjects are matters that might well be discussed in conference. There has not anything arisen between your Corporation and the employees whom we represent in which the question of "the closed shop" has been even mooted.

We read with great care your statement as to the interest the Corporation takes in the lives and welfare of the employees and their families, and if that were true even in a minor degree, we would not be pressing consideration, through a conference, of the terrible conditions that exist. The conditions of employment, the home life, the misery in the hovels of the steel workers is beyond description. You may not be aware that the standard of life of the average steel worker is below the pauper line, which means that charitable institutions furnish to the pauper a better home, more food, clothing, light and heat than many steel workers can bring into their lives upon the compensation received for putting forth their very best efforts in the steel industry. Surely this is a matter which might well be discussed in conference.

You also made reference to the attitude of your Corporation in not opposing or preventing your employees from joining labor organizations. It is a matter of common knowledge that the tactics employed by your Corporation and subsidiaries have for years most effectively prevented any attempt at organization by your employees. We feel that a conference would be valuable to your Corporation for the purpose of getting facts of which, judging from your letter, you seem to be misinformed.

Some few days are still at the disposal of our committee before the time limit will have expired when there will be no discretion left to the committee but to enforce the decree of your employees whom we have the honor to represent.

We submit that reason and fairness should obtain rather than that the alternative shall be compulsory upon us.

Surely reasonable men can find a common ground upon which we can all stand and prosper.

If you will communicate with us further upon this entire matter, please address your communication to the National Hotel, Washington, D.C., where we will be Thursday and Friday, August 28 and 29.

Very truly yours,
JOHN FITZPATRICK
D. J. DAVIS
WM. HANNON
EDW. J. EVANS
WM. Z. FOSTER
Committee

No reply came to the last letter. Mr. Gary, behind the smoke screen of his hypocrisies about the "open shop," was determined to have the strike go on. But the committee, fully conscious of the tremendous responsibility resting upon it, was equally decided to exhaust every possible means of adjustment before things came to a rupture. The committeemen went to Washington, appeared before the Executive Council of the A.F. of L., and received its endorsement and praise for the manner in which the campaign had been conducted.

Mr. Gompers was delegated by the Council to go with the committee to present the matter to President Wilson, and to request him to arrange a conference with the steel people.

When President Wilson was informed of the true situation of the steel industry, that all the men were asking for was a conference at which to present their grievances—absolutely no other demand having been made upon Mr. Gary—he immediately admitted the justice of the committee's position. He stated frankly that he was entirely out of sympathy with employers who refused to meet with representatives of their workers for the purpose of bargaining collectively on labor conditions, and he definitely agreed to use all his influence privately to have Mr. Gary alter his decision and to arrange the conference....

A week passed, with no word from the President. Conditions in the steel industry were frightful. The companies, realizing the importance of striking the first blow, were discharging men by the thousands. The unions could wait no longer. They had to move or be annihilated....

The international presidents met on September 9. A telegram from Secretary Tumulty was laid before them, to the effect that President Wilson had not yet been successful in arranging the requested conference; that he was somewhat discouraged, but was continuing his efforts. The general opinion took this to be final, that Mr. Gary had definitely refused the President's request. But in order to make assurance doubly sure and to convince all involved that everything possible had been done to avert a break, . . [a] further telegram was sent to Mr. Wilson, over the objections of some who felt it was practically asking him to declare the strike....

On the day following, Secretary Tumulty's answer was laid on the table before the meeting, practically repeating what his first telegram had said....

. . . Accordingly President Tighe of the Amalgamated Association moved that the strike be set for September 22. His motion was unanimously adopted. The die was cast....

Then came a bolt from the blue. Next morning the newspapers carried a telegram from Secretary Tumulty to President Gompers requesting that the strike be held off until after the Industrial conference, beginning October 6. The committeemen could hardly believe their eyes, because the telegram they had received from Mr. Tumulty had said absolutely nothing about postponing the strike....

. . . Before the Committee lay two requests to postpone the strike; one from President Wilson, clear and categoric; the other from Mr. Gompers, qualified by the hope that it could be done "without injury to the workers and their cause." To deny these powerful requests meant to be accused, in the first instance, of hasty and disloyal action, and in the second, of practical revolt against the officials of the A.F. of L. It would be to start the strike under the handicap of an unduly hostile public opinion. Yet to grant them meant ruin complete.

Conditions in the steel industry were desperate. Everywhere the employers were making vigorous attacks on the unions....

In the face of this situation it would have been folly to have the steel workers abandon their strike preparations, even if it could have been done. It was like asking one belligerent to ground arms in the face of its onrushing antagonist. The employers gave not the slightest sign of a truce. Long before anything could be hoped for from the Industrial conference, they would have cut the unions to pieces, had the workers been foolish enough to give them the opportunity.

This the steel workers were determined not to do. Immediately after the story got abroad that the strike might be postponed, they met in their unions and notified the National Committee that they were going to strike on September 22, regardless of anything that body might do short of getting them definite concessions and protection. Many long weary months they had waited patiently, under the urgings of the organizers, for a chance to redress their grievances. And now when they had built their organizations; taken their strike vote; received their strike call and were ready to deliver a blow at their oppressors, the opportunity of a generation was at hand, and they were not going to see it lost. They would not postpone indefinitely, and in all likelihood break up altogether, the movement they had suffered so much to build, in the vague hope that the Industrial conference, which they had no guarantee would even consider their case, and which was dominated by their arch enemies, Gary and Rockefeller, would in some distant day do something for them. Their determination to have the strike go on was intensified by the constant ding-donging of the Steel Trust propaganda in the mills to the effect that the A.F. of L. unions were cowardly and corrupt; that they would make no fight for the steel workers, and that a postponement of the strike would be proof positive that they had sold out. . . .

Between certain, ignominious defeat and possible victory, or at the worst honorable failure, the National Committee had only one choice. Practically all the delegates present were of the opinion that the strike had to go on . . . the Conference Committee addressed a long letter to President Wilson, . . . The letter closed as follows:

Mr. President, delay is no longer possible. We have tried to find a way but cannot. We regret that for the first time your call upon Organized Labor cannot meet with favorable response. Believe us the fault is not ours. If delay were no more than delay, even at the cost of loss of membership in our organizations, we would urge the same to the fullest of our ability, notwithstanding the men are set for an immediate strike. But delay here means the surrender of all hope. This strike is not at the call of the leaders, but that of the men involved. Win or lose, the strike is inevitable and will continue until industrial despotism will recede from the untenable position now occupied by Mr. Gary. We have faith in your desire to bring about a conference and hope you will succeed therein. We fully understand the hardships that meanwhile will follow and the reign of terror that unfair employers will institute. The burden falls upon the men, but the great responsibility therefor rests upon the other side. . . .

. . . Everywhere the steel companies made gigantic preparations to crush their aspiring workers back to slavery. The newspapers shrieked revolution. The whole country was atremble with anxiety and apprehension. . . .

Pittsburgh was the storm center. There, in its stronghold, the Steel Trust went ahead with strike-breaking measures unprecedented in industrial history. It provisioned and fortified its great mills and furnaces, surrounding them with stockades topped off with heavily charged electric wires, and bristling with machine guns. It assembled whole armies of gunmen. . . .

Western Pennsylvania is controlled body and soul by the Steel Trust. The whole district has the psychology of a company-owned town. . . .

Despite all these terroristic methods the Steel Trust could not break the will of its workers. On September 22 they struck throughout the entire industry with a discipline and universality that will be remembered so long as steel is made in America. On Tuesday, the twenty-third, 304,000 had quit their posts in the mills and furnaces. All week their ranks were augmented until by September 30, there were 365,600 on strike. It was a magnificent effort for freedom, and twice as big a strike as this country had ever known. . . .

The shutdown was almost complete. Throughout the country the industry was stricken with paralysis. On an average the strike was at least 90 per cent effective. . . .

For the most part the great walkout was concentrated on the smelting and rolling branches of the steel industry. . . .

Although the United States Steel Corporation was recognized as the arch enemy of the unions, the strike was not directed against it alone. Every iron and steel mill and furnace in the country not working under union agreements was included. . . .

The great steel strike thoroughly exposed the hypocrisies of Mr. Gary and his ilk that in some mysterious way labor policies and conditions in the steel industry depend upon the wishes of the body of the workers. It made plain that in the autocratic system now prevailing the democratic principles of majority and minority do not enter. It is a case pure and simple of the absolute sway of property rights over human rights. A handful of social parasites hidden away in Wall Street, with no other interest in the steel industry than to exploit it, settle arbitrarily the vital questions of wages, hours and working conditions, while the enormous mass of the workers, actual producers whose very lives are involved, have no say whatsoever. No matter how bitter their grievances, when they raise their voice to ask redress, they are discharged, blacklisted, starved, beaten, jailed and even shot, until they bend the knee again and yield to the will of their industrial masters. . . .

Elbert H. Gary: PRINCIPLES AND POLICIES OF THE UNITED STATES STEEL CORPORATION

ADVERSE, even harsh, criticisms have sometimes been made with reference to the treatment of employes; but in this connection it is noticeable that these criticisms have generally originated with, or been supported by, ill-advised or vicious-minded outsiders and not by the workmen themselves. We do not ignore criticism. If it is justified, we seek for and apply a proper remedy.

During the twenty years of our existence there has not been material hostility shown or serious complaint made to the management by our workmen themselves, either individually or in committees or groups formed by them (as permitted by our practice), which has not been cheerfully considered by the management and promptly disposed of to the mutual satisfaction of both parties.

Obviously it is for the pecuniary interests of both employer and employe to avoid controversy and to maintain peaceful and satisfactory relations. No outsider could or would be as solicitous for the welfare of the employe as the employer, nor for the employer as the employe. Success for both depends upon friendly relations; failure for both results from hostility. Both realize this and, in the present age, act accordingly, unless unduly influenced by outsiders who, from personal and unworthy motives or from a desire to attract public attention or from misguided zeal or lack of experience and information, are misled into a position which is harmful and unjustified.

As a result of these conditions, misrepresentations are made; some with good intentions, but more frequently from improper motives.

The management of the Steel Corporation has steadfastly striven to cultivate a feeling of amity with the workmen and has been very successful.

And we insist with emphasis that the employes of the Corporation, on the average, have received as high, if not the highest, compensation, and as generous, if not the most generous, treatment accorded by any basic industry at any period in this or any other country.

At the same time we claim that the rates which have been paid have not been higher, or the treatment given any more liberal, than the workmen have deserved or than was wise and proper from the standpoint of the shareholder's interest.

Labor Unions

Connected with the consideration of the treatment of labor is the question of "Labor Unions."

As stated and repeated publicly, we do not combat, though we do not contract or deal with, labor unions as such. Personally, I believe they may have been justified in the long past, for I think the workmen were not always treated justly; that because of their lack of experience or otherwise they were unable to protect

From Elbert H. Gary, *Statement at Annual Meeting of Stockholders*, April 18, 1921, pp. 9–17, 19–22. Used by permission.

themselves; and therefore needed the assistance of outsiders in order to secure their rights.

But whatever may have been the conditions of employment in the long past, and whatever may have been the results of unionism, concerning which there is at least much uncertainty, there is at present, in the opinion of the large majority of both employers and employes, no necessity for labor unions; and that no benefit or advantage through them will accrue to anyone except the union labor leaders.

In discussing the question of labor unions it should be always borne in mind what is commonly unknown or overlooked or, at least, minimized, that—

In the United States not more than ten to fifteen percent of labor is, or was at its highest point during the war, actually included in the membership of the unions. Also that the workmen do not voluntarily join the unions, do not seek the opportunity, do not search for leaders to form and maintain organizations; and on the contrary, that self-appointed leaders, who expect to receive pecuniary profit, have been and are constantly and persistently soliciting the workmen to become members. These leaders create and maintain the organizations at the expense of those who are actually workmen and join through intimidation, over-persuasion, false promises, misrepresentation or because of the use of other vicious or unworthy methods.

Recent published statements aver that there has been established an enormous fund to carry on the work of the labor union leaders, and that it is proposed to enter upon a vigorous and costly campaign for enlarging labor unions. What work shall be done, what amounts shall be collected or expended, what salaries shall be paid to leaders, will supposedly be determined by the union leaders. I have never heard of books being kept or accounts rendered to the rank and file. It is the common belief that the workmen, as a rule, know nothing and have little to say in management of the affairs of the unions.

Therefore, it is plain that the public speaker or writer who assumes that the union labor leaders represent "Labor" as a class is mistaken—first, because a comparatively small percentage of labor is connected with the unions, and, secondly, because a relatively small number of the members of the unions actually participate in any action taken. Of course, under some circumstances, as the result of coercion, threats, insults or wild promises, members of the unions, not previously consulted, may and do temporarily join a movement precipitated by the leaders and thus for a time nominally increase the membership.

If a workman desires to join a labor union he is, of course, at liberty to do so, and in that case he should not be discriminated against by an "open shop" so long as he respects the rights of his employer and his co-employes and in every way conforms to the laws of the land. The "open shop," as heretofore publicly defined is what we believe in and stand for.

But still, our opinion is that the existence and conduct of labor unions, in this country at least, are inimical to the best interests of the employes, the employers and the general public. It has been claimed that a large number of the leaders, including the most influential, are foreign born.

Union leaders perhaps may, for it is common, dispute some of the claims we make, but if so any one can, for himself or herself, inquire of both employers and employes, and will I believe ascertain that conditions applying to union labor are even much worse than now described.

If a workman desires to engage in work and remain in an establishment which is operating under contracts with union labor, that is through the leaders, he must first join the union and pay whatever dues are demanded. Sometimes they are rather high. If he should be employed without being previously questioned he would soon be approached by a "walking delegate" and ordered to join the union or quit work. If he refused and the employer declined to discharge him he would, in usual cases, be assaulted publicly, or more probably under cover of darkness; and perhaps the members of his family would be insulted or threatened, or both. If still the employer refused to interfere, he also would be subject to similar treatment, perhaps including damage to person or property. Finally, a strike would likely be called by the leaders regardless of the demand for the products in question or the necessities for wages on the part of the workmen. Should the employer fill the shops with other men then, to the extent the lack of police protection existed, force would be resorted to by the unions. These conditions might not apply in all cases, but they are at least common.

The fact is that usually union labor leaders persuade, if possible, but if they fail in this they resort to force. That there are exceptional men of different attitude may be admitted. I do not deal in personalities. It is for you and all others interested to ascertain, if not already advised, what is the rule, and what are the facts in individual cases. Look, listen and read if you are not already informed concerning these matters.

If the workman referred to accedes to the demand to join the union then what happens? He pays the dues required and the assessments made from time to time by the leaders. He works where and when the employer decides, *provided only*, the union consents. He must live up to the rules, instructions and conditions of the leader. The hours must not exceed the number consented to by the leader and the output of the workman must not exceed the limit fixed by him. In transportation the distance traveled is also limited. However skillful the workman may be or become he cannot be promoted to a better job or position except for seniority in time of employment. That is the general rule. He may labor for months or years in a low wage or salary position, though entitled by skill to earn a much larger amount. He cannot advance on merit. He is an instrument, a tool, of the union. If, for some trivial cause, or even an immoral one, such as the discharge of a law-breaking fellow employe, a strike is called, this particular workman must quit even though his family is in need of the compensation he would receive if working.

The workman, if he belongs to a labor union, becomes the industrial slave of the union. He has no power of initiative or opportunity to apply his natural mental and physical capacity. If our own shops should become thoroughly unionized and all others likewise should recognize the unions, and the steel industry should become entirely organized, as the leaders have openly attempted, then the management would be in the hands of the unions. Some of you have, no doubt, personally seen or read of the results of complete organization by the unions in certain lines.

The natural and certain effects of labor unionism are expressed by three words: Inefficiency, high costs. And be it remembered that in the end the general public, which is more interested in the selling prices of all products, must pay for extortionate, unnecessary and unreasonable costs of production. It is primarily, fundamentally and finally interested in the existence and conduct of labor unions.

I am not discussing what is the fair proportion or division of the proceeds of business, between capital, labor and consumer. I am referring to the subject of waste, of unreasonable, unconscionable, unjustified conditions and terms which restrict and hamper natural, orderly, legitimate and sensible management and progress.

The end sought by labor union leaders that, at least to which their efforts tend, means disaster and destruction.

It is noticeable that oftentimes they seek to control politics, and openly, as a body, advocate the election or defeat of even the President of the United States. They oppose or favor legislation of divers kinds. They would regulate police departments. They would, if possible, fill all official positions and control the existence, repeal or change of laws. Worse than everything else, they would dominate the Supreme Court of the United States, our citadel of defense to person and property—to civilization itself. Many of them criticize and defy the final decisions of the courts. Very little has been written or spoken concerning this attitude, although it strikes at the very foundation of our great Republic.

I would not intentionally do an injustice to any union labor leader, nor to a labor union. But I firmly believe complete unionization of the industry of this country, as attempted, would be the beginning of industrial decay.

I have been informed of many facts concerning the intentions and efforts of union labor leaders in seeking, and, in some cases, securing, control of vital departments of industry, where possession of a small unit would mean obstruction to many other larger ones; of various devices to prevent the usual course of trade movements without apparently trying to interfere with the larger and better known agencies. Some of you know of these things. You have seen them even in small repairs or restorations in your own business places or homes. Many believe the labor union leaders, or some of them, would control even the public press by unionizing the typographical departments and thus bringing about censorship of publications. Such as these would, if possible, control the speech of clergymen or public teachers. They would undoubtedly expend money to employ individuals to obtain and publish misinformation that might improperly influence the public, including teachers of high standing and repute. It has been alleged that just at present there is a secret, persistent movement, more dangerous, possibly more effective, to secure control of various agencies of information in the direction of extending unionism.

If any individual is without information in regard to any of these matters, he or she should ascertain the facts so that no mistake will be made nor injustice done. Inquire as to the result of labor unions abroad.

It seems to me that the natural, if not the necessary, result of the contemplated progress of labor unions, if successful, would be to secure the control of shops, then of the general management of business, then of capital, and finally of government. . . .

Days and Hours of Work

The Corporation inherited the twelve-hour day and the seven-day week system for necessary continuous operations. They had been and still are in vogue in many lines of industry in various countries. Perhaps they will never be entirely abolished. Possibly the workmen themselves, the employers or the general public will never, as a whole, consent to the entire elimination of either proposition. From an economic viewpoint, there is much to be said in favor of the existence of both, particularly the twelve-hour day. Many departments of industry, from a practicable consideration, require continuous operation. However, you are entitled to know the attitude of the corporate managers concerning these matters. . . .

Although the officials of the Steel Corporation and of the subsidiary companies have devoted much time to the twelve-hour-day question, we have not as yet been able to reach a conclusion. Our principal difficulty arises from the fact that the workmen themselves are unwilling to have the hours of labor decreased for the reason that they desire the larger weekly compensation resulting from the longer hours. We are not ignorant of the fact that there is more or less public sentiment against the twelve-hour day; and if it were practicable we would be glad to lessen the hours throughout our entire organization. We do not, however, endorse the claim sometimes made by public speakers that we should ignore the wishes of our employes in this respect; nor do we feel certain that twelve hours per day in all cases is necessarily injurious or objectionable. The officers of our respective subsidiary companies who are most in favor of permitting work of twelve hours per day where the work is necessarily continuous are those who have heretofore personally been employed twelve hours per day or more, either in the shops or on the farms, and have reached their present higher positions by reason of their demonstrated ability and success.

The officers of the Corporation, the presidents of subsidiary companies and

a majority of others in positions of responsibility are in favor of abolishing the twelve-hour day, and for this reason and because of the public sentiment referred to, it is our endeavor and expectation to decrease the working hours—we hope in the comparatively near future. We have been disappointed by our inability heretofore to accomplish our purpose in this regard.

Collective Bargaining

You have read or heard these words. Whatever may be the general conception of the term, we have given the subject, as we understand it, much consideration.

So far as I am informed, our employes have not requested the adoption of a plan for collective action different from the practice in vogue throughout our companies. Outsiders have occasionally offered suggestions. They have been made by three different groups.

First, by the labor union leaders who mean by the term, and openly seek to bring about, collective bargaining directly through the labor unions or in such a manner as to secure control of the workmen through the unions, and thus force all the workmen into membership. This, in all their efforts, is the one principal thing sought to be achieved. They oppose openly every kind of collective bargaining that is contrary in form or practice to this idea.

Second, persons who are really acting in the interest of the labor unions, are or have been members, or at least, believe in them and advocate their existence. Many of them, I think, are disingenuous, to say the least, and purposely conceal their real wishes and intentions.

Third, a number of public speakers or writers who are able, honest and sincere, believing that workmen, in some cases at least, would be benefited by collective action concerning terms and conditions of employment.

From our inquiry and study we do not believe any plan for collective bargaining has been put in practice which is better than our own, or has been of real benefit to the employe or employer. On the contrary, it seems to us that experience, up to date, shows that both have been disadvantaged; that there has been less efficiency and higher cost, and that therefore the great consuming public has been injured.

As a matter of fact, according to our information, all the modern collective bargaining plans were adopted under conditions or in times of emergency and on the real, if not disclosed, ground that they were "the lesser of two evils"; that they would perhaps prevent the unionization of the plants in question. Indeed, the labor unions themselves openly objected to and argued against these plans for these reasons. If, or to the extent this objection has been withdrawn or modified, it is obviously because it is believed by the union labor leaders that the collective bargaining plans in force have not been hostile to, but rather an aid to the labor unions.

However, it is proper to say that if a plan, better than ours, is developed and proven to be of real benefit to the employes and, at the same time reasonable, practicable and fair to them, we will not be slow to adopt it.

We do not endorse experimentation, especially concerning workmen, unless it seems practical and reasonable. I venture the individual opinion that any plan which seeks to deprive the investor of the control of his property and business is inimical to the fundamental ideas of our country and to the public welfare. Any step in this direction is to be deplored. Any nation which adopts it will fail to maintain a leading position in industrial proficiency and progress. A man, or group of men, contending for a different attitude, is opposing self-protection and interest.

It is a fair and wise conclusion that anyone claiming the right to a voice in the management of the property of a corporation should do so through a stockholding interest, and thus share responsibility and liability and profits with all other stockholders.

Nevertheless, we believe that the employe should not only be treated fairly and justly up to the full measure of practicability, but that he should have the chance to consult as to all terms of employment, either as an individual or in groups of workmen in any department. This has been and is our plan and it has proved to be beneficial and satisfactory to both employer and employe.

Thus our employes in groups, or as individuals, at all times, have access to the office of the foreman or to any other superior officer, even to the highest.

We do not look with favor upon the request for an interview concerning our employes by a volunteer outsider, representing only himself or his own selfish interests, and who is known to be actually hostile to both the employer and employe, or to the country.

It is the unqualified, undeviating policy of our Corporation to be polite to everyone. Our instructions to this effect to our whole organization are positive and binding. We are not defiant, combative or inconsiderate.

In closing, I emphasize the fact that the presidents and other officers and managers of our subsidiary companies are able, conscientious, altogether worthy, and in harmony with the policies I have stated. They are entitled to much credit for the great value of our properties and the success of our enterprise.

Elbert H. Gary: TESTIMONY BEFORE THE SENATE INVESTIGATING COMMITTEE

THE Committee on Education and Labor of the United States Senate met, pursuant to the call of the chairman, in room 235, Senate Office Building, Hon. William S. Kenyon presiding. . . .

THE CHAIRMAN. We would like to hear from you as to the genesis of this strike, the questions involved as you see them, and everything about it.

MR. GARY. I suppose you know my business connections?

THE CHAIRMAN. Yes; but probably it would be well for you to make that clear in the record.

MR. GARY. I am the chairman of the board of directors, chairman of the finance committee, and chief executive officer of the United States Steel Corporation in general charge of its affairs. . . .

It has been well known for several years, more especially during the last two years, that the labor unions were attempting, in their own way, to organize the employees of the subsidiary companies of the United States Steel Corporation. That has been frequently and publicly announced.

It has been stated on this floor, before this honorable committee, that the subsidiary companies of the United States Steel Corporation have been guilty of ill treatment of their employees, and some statements made before the committee have been based on misinformation and are absolutely without foundation.

I wish to state, Mr. Chairman and gentlemen, that there is no basic industry in this country, nor in the world, in my opinion, which has paid larger wages to its employees than the United States Steel Corporation, and perhaps not as large; nor treated its employees with greater respect and consideration than the United States Steel Corporation and its subsidiaries, if as great. . . .

It has been charged that during the impending strike the subsidiary companies have been guilty of attacking and mistreating the strikers. That is entirely without foundation. There is not a vestige of truth in that statement.

Three instances have been mentioned by a former witness. A photograph was displayed, I think before this committee, and it was said a woman was killed by representatives of a subsidiary company. . . .

Mrs. Fannie Snellings was shot at a place called Brackenridge, in Pennsylvania. We have no works there; no men there.

If she was killed at that place, concerning which I have no contradiction to make, it was by people other than anyone connected with any subsidiary of the United States Steel Corporation or with the corporation itself, or with the knowledge of any of them. . . .

SENATOR JONES. What was the cause of that disturbance?

MR. GARY. Strikers were, as I understand, attacking coal miners and some of

From *Hearings before the Committee on Education and Labor, U. S. Senate, Sixty-sixth Congress, Pursuant to S. Res. 202* (Washington, Government Printing Office, 1919), pp. 145–148, 150–154, 161, 163–164, 166–168, 173–175, 206–208, 215–219.

those in charge of the mine fired shots at the strikers, who were attacking them in the usual way, and I presume you know what that is—by the use of brickbats, clubs, and guns, and almost anything else; and in defending themselves, we are informed, the employees there did fire some shots. I have not read this to see what the verdict finds, but the shot in question was probably fired by the strikers themselves. I think that is the consensus of opinion and the belief, as I have been informed. . . .

MR. GARY. . . . Another witness testified in regard to Mr. Jefferson Davis Pierce, of Worcester, Mass. . . .

The son of this man, Jefferson Davis Pierce, Jr., having seen an account of this testimony in the newspapers, brought to our offices September 27 an affidavit which he had prepared himself, and which I will read with your permission. . . .

"I was with my father the night he received his injuries in Monessen, Pa., and wish to state very emphatically that his injury was not caused by any one connected with the United States Steel Corporation. On the contrary, it was caused by a member of the I. W. W. organization from out of town, who was sent there at the time to create trouble, as the I. W. W. organization was then trying to gain control of the organizing situation. . . ."

MR. GARY. . . .

Another witness, I think, testified to a number of deaths and injuries at Hammond, Ind. We had nothing whatever to do with the trouble or the strike at that place. We have no business of any kind, no interests there. . . .

MR. GARY. . . . This strike has been conducted in many respects like other strikes, only worse in some of its features. The large majority of our workmen were not desirous of engaging in a strike. They were not members of any labor union; they had declined to become such, year after year. . . .

. . . This strike was inaugurated by the union leaders, not by the men. The union leaders have been attempting all these years to organize the men. The men have not been seeking the assistance of anyone to organize them. . . .

* * *

. . . Strikes were threatened from time to time; there have been a great many threats by union leaders, going back over quite a long period. They say we obstructed their movements, we interfered with their program. If we did it was because we treated our men in such a way that they preferred to remain outside of the unions. But the strike was anticipated by threats, intimidations and promises of various kinds which might appeal to the natural cupidity of uneducated workmen. I have several specimens with me, a good many specimens—I will say a number of specimens that have been sent to me—of letters sent to the families of the workmen, which I will produce for the inspection of the Senators if desired.

Well, the strike was called. The threats had been made, we do not know how many, we have a great deal of hearsay testimony on that subject—statements made by families—of threats to burn their houses, to blow up their houses, to kidnap their children, to kill the workmen, and so forth and so forth; and when the strike was called large numbers of men, if we may believe them in their statements made at the time and that have been made since, remained away from their working places because they were afraid to go, and because they did not believe the protection furnished by the State or cities or the sheriffs was adequate. After the protection had been furnished in many places the men have commenced to return to their shops. Now, if you include all the men who remained away from their shops after the strike was called, I think it is a fair statement to say not over 28 per cent of the total employees of the subsidiary companies of the United States Steel Corporation were out, remained away. But if you limit that to the manufacturing companies where the strikes have actually been pending, it might have been as high as 40 per cent at one time. I will say that is the outside figure, and we have taken considerable pains to ascertain the facts in relation to it.

SENATOR STERLING. Now, Mr. Gary, this figure of 28 per cent which you have stated, would that include not only those men who actually struck but those who remained at home because of fear for their safety?

MR. GARY. Yes, it would....

* * *

MR. GARY. ... The men were not complaining; the workmen had found no fault. We are on the best of terms with our men and have always been, with some very slight exceptions, very inconsequential exceptions....

SENATOR WALSH. Was there any other reason for your refusal to hear these men, to see whether they did represent your men or not, except that your personal investigation satisfied you that they could not enlighten you any about the condition of your workmen and their relationship to your company?

MR. GARY. Well, I want to be frank enough to say that it has been my policy, and the policy of our corporation, not to deal with union labor leaders.

SENATOR WALSH. Any way, at any time?

MR. GARY. At any time. And for the

reason we do not believe in contracting with unions. When an employer contracts with the union labor leaders he immediately drives all of his employees into the unions. Otherwise, they can not get employment. That is a part of the reason for trying to organize the men, and that is why we have been such an obstruction. I am not antagonizing unions, I am not saying that they have not a perfect right to form unions, of course they have; but we are not obliged to contract with them if we do not choose to do so; and we think, because of many things that have happened—and some of them are happening today—that unionism is not a good thing for the employer or employee today, either one, any more than the man who does belong to a union should be prohibited from working in our shop.

SENATOR WALSH. Is it not practically setting up an opposition to unions to refuse to meet and talk over labor conditions with their representatives?

MR. GARY. Well, I don't think so, Senator.

SENATOR WALSH. Is it not practically notice to every employee that the officials of the company do not recognize and do not want unions in their establishments?

MR. GARY. Well, I can not quite concede that, Senator, although I will concede that it is notice to the men that we do not contract with the unions.

SENATOR WALSH. Yet you say that the men have a right to unionize.

MR. GARY. Of course they have.

SENATOR WALSH. What good is the right to unionizing if the leaders or representatives can not talk with their employers? What is the use of a union if the leaders of the men can not talk to the employers? Is it simply a social society?

MR. GARY. I do not think the leader

should undertake to talk with the employers—of a few of the men in a shop —when they know in advance that no contracts are made with the union labor leaders, and especially when the men themselves are not requesting it. Now these men say—they have said here that the men were requesting them. . . .

SENATOR BORAH. . . . Will you state what you conceive to be the fundamental issue or the moral question which you said was involved which you could arbitrate?

MR. GARY. Well, Senator, the fundamental issue, as I conceive it, is the question of an open shop or a closed shop, the question of allowing a man to work where he pleases, whether he belongs to a union or not, and the right of an employer to employ a man in his shop whether the man is a union man or is not. I believe that it is well known all over the world and is the opinion of a large majority of the people of the world that the open shop is essential to progress and prosperity, and that the closed shop means less production, less work, higher costs.

I think, when you are discussing the question of the high cost of living, there is nothing more important to consider with it than that manufacturing establishments shall be allowed to operate, unrestricted by labor unions or anybody else, depending upon the good will of the laborers, the workmen themselves, who of course are controlled by the treatment they receive, including wage rates and working and living conditions. . . .

* * *

MR. GARY. Now, as to the moral issue: I think it is immoral for a small minority of men, organized if you please, to compel by force a large majority to yield to their desires and to submit to their control. Because if the industries of this country or any other were controlled by union labor, as it would be if these gentlemen are successful—and I am not dealing in personalities—it would mean decay, less production, higher cost; and this country could not succeed in its contest with other countries for the world's business, it would be in the condition that I fear England is in today, but which I hope it will come out of.

Now, I think when a few men, comparatively speaking, seek to impose their will to forcibly secure control of a business against the wishes of a large majority, that is immoral. That is my opinion of that. And here were outsiders, bear in mind, rank outsiders, who stated publicly away back at the St. Paul meeting, and it was testified to here before this committee, that they were starting out to organize the steel industry, which they had failed to accomplish in the past; that was their view; not for the purpose of securing better pay, better conditions; none of the twelve points which have been made since this strike was called, I think, was mentioned. We have never heard anything about those twelve points; none of our men have made any complaint; but these men were forcing themselves into the steel business, to unionize it all and to get control of it. And what would happen if they got control of it? Is there any man here who has had any experience with organized labor who does not know? . . .

SENATOR BORAH. Without assuming to argue the question one way or the other, if labor can not deal with the great industries of the country collectively, do you think that it would be practical or practicable or possible for labor to maintain itself and its rights, its wages and so forth, as against combined capitalism? Can labor deal with capital without dealing with it in the same way, combined and collectively?

MR. GARY. I think labor can deal collectively and it ought to be encouraged to deal collectively, and it ought not to be prohibited at any time from dealing collectively; but dealing collectively, in the form of committees, or however they themselves may decide, is one thing, and dealing collectively as insisted upon by the labor union leaders, which means that the union labor leaders shall decide all these questions, and shall represent the men, whether they are asked to or not, and will establish a basis for the closed shop which would shut out the individual voices of these men practically, is quite a different thing. . . .

SENATOR JONES (of New Mexico). . . . It has been intimated that these men, if they come with grievances, or attempt to organize, that they are in a sense blacklisted, and that sooner or later some excuse is trumped up for their discharge.

MR. GARY. Senator, there is no foundation in fact for that assertion. . . .

SENATOR MCKELLAR. You said a while ago, as I understood you, that you favored collective bargaining on the part of labor. Is that carried out in your shops, or what are the facts in reference to it?

MR. GARY. The collective bargaining spoken of, some of those who have adopted a practice which is so referred to say that is really a misnomer. It is not important whether that is so or not. There has been adopted, commencing with the Colorado Fuel & Iron, two or three years ago, not to be specific, what I think they termed collective bargaining. Some of you, particularly Senator Phipps, will know more about that than I. Other companies, like the Midvale, the Youngstown Sheet & Tube and the Inland Steel, have adopted a form of shop committees, shop committee work. Now, we are watching those with a great deal of interest, a great deal of concern. One of the propositions of the labor unions, one of the 12 demands, is that they shall be abolished, and those who have adopted the shop committee plan say it is because it interferes with labor unions, that labor unions can not succeed with that as a substitute. Some of the men, I understand, have been dissatisfied with them in some respects, I do not know what, but I do know the Colorado Fuel men are out on strike now, or part of them at least, and also some of the Bethlehem, I do not know how many: they say a small number; others claim a large number. Practically all of the Midvale people at Cambria, 15,000 men, are out. The Inland Steel men are all out; and it would seem there may be dissatisfaction on the part of some of them; that is, a part of those men at least have joined labor unions and have heeded the call. I know nothing about it, although it is reported to us that those men, in large numbers, are now anxious to get back and are trying to get back into the shops, but are prohibited by the strikers. . . .

. . . We try to find out what our men really want, and then if it is practicable and just put it into effect. We were not asked during the last few years to increase the wages of our men at any time, as far as I know not a single time; and we increased them over and over again. Why? Because we thought they were entitled to it on the merits. We have always done that. We have stood for the highest wages invariably. We have been the first to increase wages and the last to decrease them. In fact, I think we have decreased our wages but once since our company was organized in 1901, and we have increased them 10 or a dozen or 15 times; and as I have shown, they have been trebled—and on the merits. Consequently we have not had much if any complaint from our men. . . .

THE CHAIRMAN. You are familiar with the policies enunciated by the National War Labor Board, are you not, Judge?

MR. GARY. Well, to some extent. I am not particularly acquainted with those conditions or facts.

THE CHAIRMAN. I notice in the "Principles and policies to govern relations between workers and employers in war industries for the duration of the war," this proposition is laid down:

Right to organize. The right of workers to organize in trade-unions and to bargain collectively through chosen representatives is recognized and affirmed. This right shall not be denied, abridged, or interfered with by the employers in any manner whatsoever.

Did you subscribe to any such doctrine as that for war times?

MR. GARY. It depends upon what you mean by collective bargaining. If you mean the collective bargaining that the unions are now claiming to insist upon, we did not. If you mean the right of men through committees to present their questions, or any question, yes, in principle. We had nothing to do with the War Labor Board.

THE CHAIRMAN. You had nobody from your plant connected with it at all?

MR. GARY. No.

THE CHAIRMAN. Well, the right to organize in trade-unions—you do not endorse that policy, do you?

MR. GARY. No—well, the right to organize—I do endorse that. I do not combat or contest that. I think laboring people have a perfect right to join a union, and I think anybody has a right to form a union.

SENATOR JONES. Judge Gary, I understood Mr. Fitzpatrick to state here the other day that they were not seeking to organize all of the men of the Steel Corporation into the union and have it what is known as a "union shop"; that that was not the issue at all, and I understand now that you substantially put yourself on the same plane, you do not object to these men belonging to labor unions, if I understand you correctly.

MR. GARY. That is right.

SENATOR JONES. And the other parties are not insisting that all of your employees shall be members of a labor union, and I should like to know, with those views in mind, what is the difference here between you and the representatives of labor unions.

MR. GARY. The difference, first, is in the statement of facts. The labor unions secure as many of the employees in every line of industry as they can to join their unions. It is a misstatement of fact to say that they only desire or seek to secure a number of members. When they can succeed and they have the power by reason of the numbers of employees to compel the owners to contract with them in regard to labor, as they do wherever it is possible so far as my experience and information goes, then of course nonunion members can not get work in that mill except through the unions.

I should like to have you make as full an inquiry as you can, in this country or in any other country, and find if you can where contracts are made with the unions with respect to a number of employees, with the agreement that those who do not care to join or who do not belong to the union may come in and get employment. Now, if they have such contracts as that it is a recent thing, in my opinion, and in conformity to a scheme which has been told by some of the union labor leaders whereby it was stated that they would make an agreement whereby a shop might be partly union and partly non-union, because they knew when the contract was made for a part of the employees it would be a very short time when they would get them all in, and then they would insist upon their own terms.

SENATOR WALSH. Judge Gary, let me see if I understand your position. You recognize the right of working men to organize?

MR. GARY. Yes.

SENATOR WALSH. You have no objection to unions in your plants. Is that right?

MR. GARY. I do not know what you mean by that.

SENATOR WALSH. You recognize the right of the men to form unions?

MR. GARY. Yes.

SENATOR WALSH. But you refuse to confer with the representatives of the unions?

MR. GARY. Yes.

SENATOR JONES. Judge Gary, so far as my personal sentiment is concerned, I made up my mind to base it wholly upon the record which should be made in this case, regardless of any inclinations which I might have one way or the other; but, according to the record in this case thus far, the representatives of the labor organizations have come here and they have said that this question of a closed shop was not at issue at all, and you have come here and said that you are perfectly willing to have what is known as the open shop, which shall employ both union and nonunion labor. Now, the public is interested in this subject. This strike is a disastrous thing for the public, and I think measurably perhaps disastrous to the Steel Corporation, and may affect vitally some of the men who have gone on strike; and the object in bringing about this investigation, as I take it, is to see if we can not discover some common ground on which the interests of the public may be protected and the interests likewise of the Steel Corporation and of the men themselves subserved. We are not here for the purpose of taking sides one way or the other in this matter, but we are here for the purpose of seeing if we can not find some common ground.

Now, if I understood your latter remark, that there is only one solution of this thing so far as you are concerned, we might as well end this examination here. If you mean to say that the only solution is to let this strike wear itself out, so far as I know, you are in position to carry that policy into effect; and if that is your policy now, if you have no common ground to suggest, it seems to me we might as well end this examination here. But I am seeking, if possible, to find some common ground on which we can meet and serve the interests of the public and your company and the employees as well.

MR. GARY. Senator, your statement is very clear and comprehensive. I think possibly you and I may differently interpret the public sentiment of this country, and if so you may be right and I wrong; but of course we are acting on our best judgment, believing we are as loyal and faithful in considering the rights and interests of the entire public as you are, although we are not disinterested as you are, I must admit.

Now, of course, the natural way to settle all industrial questions is to leave every one open and free to act on the basis of natural laws and regulations, so long as every one carefully observes the requirements of the law. I believe if the attitude of the public is to insist, first, upon observing the requirements of the law, of maintaining absolute peace, of preventing breaches of law and unlawful disturbances, so that every man and every interest is protected, that this whole difficulty will work out. I think people ought to be allowed to make their own agreements, their own contracts with their men. If one side or the other is transcending the rules of propriety and decency public sentiment will correct that evil. . . .

SENATOR JONES. Judge Gary, I have been of course very much impressed in hearing this statement, and it undoubtedly furnishes food for thought in connection with possible future legislation; but of course it can not become effective in a way to settle this strike. And I do not care to prolong the examination, but I would like to ask you the general question, have you any solution to suggest for the settlement of this strike?

MR. GARY. Yes.

SENATOR JONES. I should be very glad to hear it.

MR. GARY. See to it that in no place are the laws violated, that peace is continuously maintained, that individuals shall be left free to do as they please while they live up to the law; and then in that case the employees, who are the ones interested, will settle this question for themselves. Leave them to settle it. If you think at any time the employer, that is the United States Steel Corporation, is doing the wrong thing, you come and see me and satisfy me if you can, and see if it is not corrected, unless I convince you it is mistaken.

THE CHAIRMAN. You will meet the committee, will you, Judge?

MR. GARY. I certainly will. I would meet the union labor leaders, as I am meeting them to-day or as I may meet them in the General Conference. I do not call that meeting them as union labor leaders. I have nothing against them personally.

THE CHAIRMAN. I am sure they have nothing against you.

MR. GARY. Ask Mr. Gompers, ask any of them that happens to know me. I have nothing against them personally, as you know.

THE CHAIRMAN. Why was it you did not answer Mr. Gompers' letter several months ago?

MR. GARY. I thought Mr. Gompers knew perfectly well that I would not recognize him as a labor leader, he knew that by past experience, and he knew it by my answer to Mr. Tighe. If at that time I was discourteous to him I am very sorry; I did not intend it as a discourtesy.

SENATOR WALSH. Is it true, Judge, that capital has made mistakes?

MR. GARY. Do I admit it?

SENATOR WALSH. Yes.

MR. GARY. Certainly.

SENATOR WALSH. And it is true that labor has made mistakes, is it not?

MR. GARY. Why, of course.

SENATOR WALSH. Now then, when labor thinks capital has made a mistake, and capital thinks labor has made a mistake, is not the thing to do to arbitrate?

MR. GARY. It depends upon circumstances. If I should go to you, Mr. Senator, and say "I think you have made a mistake in regard to the treatment of your family," and you should deny it, and I asked for arbitration of that question, I think you would refuse.

THE CHAIRMAN. The Senator being a bachelor—(Laughter.)

SENATOR WALSH. I do not think the relationship between the employer and employee is that of a parent to his children, do you?

MR. GARY. No, I do not. But I think the relationship between the United States Steel Corporation and its employees is pretty intimate and pretty friendly, and has been growing more so year by year and day by day. I believe a large majority of our people think that we treat them fairly, not in a patronizing way, not in disregard of their rights at all, but as associates in work.

Samuel Gompers: TESTIMONY BEFORE THE SENATE INVESTIGATING COMMITTEE

THE Committee on Education and Labor of the United States Senate, pursuant to adjournment of yesterday, met at 10 o'clock a.m., in room 235, Senate Office Building, Hon. William S. Kenyon, presiding. . . .

THE CHAIRMAN. . . . What are the issues involved in this strike?

MR. GOMPERS. The issues involved in the iron and steel industry strike are varied. The right of the employees to be heard through their own representatives, through spokesmen of their own choosing; the right to have a voice in the determination of the conditions of employment, is of the most vital interest to them.

For many, many years, surely for the past 25 years, the right of association of the workers has been denied with all the power and wealth and domination of the Steel Corporation, not only through the exercise of lawful power, but directly, and more often indirectly, through denial by illegal and unwarrantable and brutal means.

. . . The right of association, the attempt to organize on the part of the working people themselves, has always met with stern opposition from the highest corporation authorities and from subordinates who carry out either the immediate direction or the understood policies of the companies.

I have not heard the testimony that has thus far been elicited before this committee, but I want to say this upon my own authority. Perhaps it may not have been presented to you: I refer to the requests which have come from the workers themselves to be organized, their appeals to us to organize them, to organize them secretly, but, in any event, to organize them. Many of the men, most of the men, who made any such effort were stopped by the detectives, by the espionage of the company agents or their detectives.

It has been elicited before committees of Congress that two years ago fully 8 per cent of the activities of detective agencies in the United States consisted in dealing with agents and detectives in the factories, shops, mills, mines, plants of employers, or in spying, watching, following, dogging men from their work to their homes, or to any place that they went; in supplying agents, or what is better known as agent provocateur to bring men into contests prematurely in order that they might commit some overt act, or that they might enter upon premature strikes for which they were unorganized and unprepared; in reporting men who had expressed some little discontent or great discontent with conditions in the plants or the mills. Men were discharged for no other reason than because of their grumbling against conditions. Men who expressed the thought or the hope that they would like to be organized or who had the temerity to go

From *Hearings before the Committee on Education and Labor, U.S. Senate, Sixty-sixth Congress, Pursuant to S. Res. 202* (Washington, Government Printing Office, 1919), pp. 87–103, 106–107, 110–112, 142–143.

to meetings in private homes or in public halls for the purpose of discussing the subject of organization were watched, tagged, and reported and the following morning would find themselves discharged.

The whole system was a greater espionage upon the workmen than was ever employed upon a man suspected of a great crime against the laws of our country or any of the States.

It was to put the fear of God into these men that if they organized or attempted to organize it would be at the peril of their employment. Being discharged from a plant of the steel industry meant practically the blacklisting of these men, and that they could not find any employment elsewhere.

SENATOR STERLING. You spoke of the right of association, of having been denied that right?

MR. GOMPERS. Yes, sir.

SENATOR STERLING. By that term do you mean that they were denied the right to organize into unions?

MR. GOMPERS. Yes; or in any other way which had a tendency to have the workers unite themselves in any form that might have an influence upon the industry, upon their employment and upon the conditions of their employment. There are quite a number of men who have not only been watched, but the meeting places, the small halls rented for the purpose of meetings have been closed against the men. The proprietors of buildings in which halls are rented have been told that they must prevent meetings being held and must have the doors locked against the men.

We know of instances of men who wanted to go to a meeting place of an organization—and this is in recent times, too—men who going from their homes to the meeting places had to pass through two lines of detectives and thugs, run the gamut of a hundred or more on each side of them. Men who met in public meetings in lofts, privately owned, who had obtained permission to hold the meetings, have been run down, charged upon, and dispersed; some of them assaulted and some of them beaten.

SENATOR STERLING. Can you give instances of that, Mr. Gompers?

MR. GOMPERS. Yes. In McKeesport quite recently.

SENATOR STERLING. Before or since the strike at McKeesport?

MR. GOMPERS. Since the strike—both before and after, and they met peaceably. I have been informed this morning, since I entered this hall, and my statement is capable of verification or refutation, that at McKeesport yesterday an order was given that no meetings can be held of the iron and steel workers in that city. The meeting halls hired for the purpose of consultation and discussion as to the situation have been closed against them. The offices of the unions of the iron and steel workers have been closed against all the men, against the officers of the local organization meeting there for the purpose of consultation as to what can be done in furtherance of the interests of the men engaged in this strike.

SENATOR STERLING. I suppose that was done, was it not, on the theory that a strike being on, the collecting of men in crowds would tend to bring about disorder and possibly violence and injury to persons and to property?

MR. GOMPERS. I do not know the theory, but I know the fact, and I think I know the purpose; and the purpose is to keep the men, the officers of the organizations, from consulting in meeting for the purpose of furthering their interests in this controversy.

In the last statement I made I said that the offices rented by the organizations of the men, in order that the representatives of these men might meet, these offices for which the rent has been paid, have been closed. That is not meeting in public, but it is the right of domicile or the right peaceably and lawfully to conduct business.

THE CHAIRMAN. Under whose orders were they closed?

MR. GOMPERS. By the order of the mayor of McKeesport. . . .

SENATOR MCKELLAR. Would you give us just the reasons why this strike was called; the grounds on which it was called, so that we can have them clearly before us; if you will just take them up in order, one after the other, and then discuss them. . . .

MR. GOMPERS. In response to the many requests to organize and to have us aid these workers in organizing, some years ago we sent a few organizers into the field. Those men were arrested and driven out of town. One of them was so bludgeoned that within a few months afterwards he died. He was one of the best, most intelligent and constructive workers and organizers in our service.

SENATOR STERLING. Was there any strike on at that time?

MR. GOMPERS. No, sir. I refer to the late Mr. Jefferson Davis Pierce, of Worcester, Mass.

SENATOR STERLING. When was that?

MR. GOMPERS. About four or five years ago. In view of the applications, made to us, we undertook a campaign of organization. We had about eight or ten of our men go among the iron and steel workers. We sent some documents printed in 22 or 23 different languages among the people calling them to meetings. The effort was abortive by reason of the tactics employed by the corporation and their representatives that I have indicated. . . .

At the convention of the American Federation of Labor, held at St. Paul, in June, 1918, a resolution or a motion was adopted, by which the officers of the various trade unions in the iron and steel industry and its various branches were called to meet during the convention. As president of the American Federation of Labor, I was named as one of those who were requested to participate in that conference, and I was present. I was elected chairman of the conference. . . .

As a consequence, at the convention of the American Federation of Labor held at Atlantic City, in June, 1919, I asked that I should be relieved from the position of chairman of the committee. I was excused, and Mr. John Fitzpatrick was elected as the chairman of that committee. . . .

SENATOR PHIPPS. Mr. Gompers, at that point, it has been stated that in the steel industry the great majority of employees are unskilled. Did this effort for organization include the unskilled workers of the steel industry?

MR. GOMPERS. Yes, sir.

SENATOR PHIPPS. And that would embrace the common day laborer, would it?

MR. GOMPERS. It would. It would include all workers employed in the iron and steel industry who had not already been organized. There are 24 national trade-unions having jurisdiction over the classes of employment, or the classes of work, rather, and of the men performing it. That class of workers for which there is no national trade-union would become directly affiliated to the American Federation of Labor.

SENATOR PHIPPS. Now, Mr. Gompers, you have expressed your opinion that while the steel corporations, that is, not only the United States Steel Corporation, but the others as well, declare that they desire to operate on an open-shop basis, their real attitude is that of limiting employment to men who will not or do not belong to unions. What is the attitude of the American Federation of Labor as regards the employment of nonunion men in shops where you have organized the employees? Is there any objection made by the federation to the employment of nonunion men?

MR. GOMPERS. The American Federation of Labor has nothing to do with the subject at all. That is a matter for the national trade unions to outline their policies.

SENATOR PHIPPS. What has been the policy as outlined by the national trade-unions?

MR. GOMPERS. The national trade-union's effort has been to try to organize the workers.

SENATOR PHIPPS. And to exclude the employment of nonunion men whenever possible?

MR. GOMPERS. To organize the workers, to try to have the workers organized in a plant 100 per cent....

SENATOR PHIPPS. ... This is President Woodrow Wilson, then signed as Dr. Woodrow Wilson, under date of January 12, 1909....

I am a fierce partisan of the open shop and of everything that makes for individual liberty, and I should like to contribute anything that might be possible for me to contribute to the clarification of thinking and the formation of right purposes in matters of this kind. ...

You know what the usual standard of the employee is in our day. It is to give as little as he may for his wages. Labor is standardized by the trades unions, and this is the standard to which it is made to conform. No one is suffered to do more than the average workman can do; in some trades and handicrafts no one is suffered to do more than the least skillful of his fellows can do within the hours allotted to a day's labor, and no one may work out of hours at all or volunteer anything beyond the minimum.

I need not point out how economically disastrous such a regulation of labor is. It is so unprofitable to the employer that in some trades it will presently not be worth his while to attempt anything at all. He had better stop altogether than operate at an inevitable and invariable loss.

The labor of America is rapidly becoming unprofitable under its present regulation by those who have determined to reduce it to a minimum.

Our economic supremacy may be lost because the country grows more and more full of unprofitable servants.

(Extracts from baccalaureate address of President Woodrow Wilson before the graduating class of Princeton University in 1909) ...

We speak too exclusively of the capitalistic class. There is another, as formidable an enemy to equality and betterment of opportunity as it is, and that is the class formed by the labor organizations and leaders of the country.

(Extract from address by Dr. Woodrow Wilson at a dinner at the Waldorf Hotel, March 18, 1918) ...

MR. GOMPERS. I think it is as unfair to quote statements made by Dr. Woodrow Wilson of 1907 and 1909 and compare them and quote them as his judgment of to-day, as it is to hold Mr. Foster, secretary of the organized committee of the iron and steel workers, for his utterances of 10 and 12 years ago, and hold him responsible for them to-day, when he has disavowed them and frankly acknowledged that he was wholly in error in his point of view at that time....

... The whole course of the President of the United States, Hon. Woodrow Wilson, in regard to labor matters, to the relations of workers to employees, to the organizations of labor, and his efforts to help to compose whatever differences existed, is in itself a sufficient answer, but let me supplement that by this—that before the war, before the United States entered into the war, he, as President of the United States, appointed the president of the American Federation of Labor as one of the advisory committee of the Council of National Defense. As President of the United States he appointed a committee of citizens, called the War Labor Conference Board, composed of five business men, organized business men, and five representatives of organized labor to meet in conference to outline policies for the adjustment of differences between employers and workers. The declarations of the conference board, with former President Taft as one of the joint chairmen and Mr. Frank P. Walsh as the other joint chairman—the declarations of that War Labor Conference Board declared for these principles. I am quoting to you from memory:

The right of collective bargaining between workers and employers.

The right of representatives of workers to be heard in any matter in controversy.

The standard eight-hour work day.

The right of a living wage for workers, conforming to the American standards of living.

THE CHAIRMAN. The right to organize into labor and to trade-unions?

MR. GOMPERS. The right to organize into trade-unions, yes, sir; and collective bargaining, and others which my memory does not now serve me. The War Labor Conference Board declarations were approved by the President of the United States, Mr. Woodrow Wilson. The personnel which constituted the War Labor Conference Board was the personnel of the War Labor Board created by the War Labor Conference Board and approved by the President of the United States, Mr. Woodrow Wilson.

At the dedication of the building of the American Federation of Labor in Washington the President of the United States, Mr. Woodrow Wilson, made the dedicatory address. I commend that address to your serious attention, Senator.

At the convention of the American Federation of Labor, held at Buffalo in November, 1917, the President of the United States, Mr. Woodrow Wilson, came to that convention and delivered an address to the delegates and visitors in attendance at that convention. I commend that address to your very serious consideration. . . .

* * *

MR. GOMPERS. In my letter and the several letters addressed to Judge Gary by the committee, there was not the remotest reference to any question of closed shop or open shop. I assert, without any hesitation or fear of contradiction, that it was not in the minds of the committee and I know it was not in the mind of myself, to discuss the question of the open and closed shop if such conference were had. It has been simply— if I may use the vulgarism—lugged in by the Judge in that letter that is read and in the publicity of the corporation that this controversy—

THE CHAIRMAN (Interrupting). Then you say that the closed shop is not an issue in this strike?

MR. GOMPERS. It is not an issue, sir. You can imagine one of the common laborers, unskilled laborers, or skilled workers, if you please, as an individual, going to Judge Gary and presenting a grievance; or, even if not to Judge Gary, to the corporation's counsel, appointed by Judge Gary. You can imagine what chance of presentation would be afforded such poor devil by the representative of this billions and millions of dollars corporation. You can imagine how much courage a man would have in appearing before Judge Gary, or one of his representatives, to present either an individual grievance or a general grievance which the workers may have.

. . .

SENATOR STERLING. . . . Do you mean to say now that the workers have no opportunity of consulting together with reference to the appointment of a committee to interview a superintendent?

MR. GOMPERS. Senator, I mean to say this, that the selection of a committee is only the second step in such a procedure. The first must be not only the feeling that the grievance exists, but the opportunity of the men to meet for the purpose of discussing those grievances and authorizing a committee, selecting a committee and authorizing it to speak on the matter for the workers and for the presentation of those grievances. I say, sir, that there is no opportunity for the workers now to discuss their real grievances with such an object in view.

SENATOR STERLING. Can you give instances here now? I do not mean during the period of a strike, when the authorities must be on the alert to quell disturbances or something of that kind; but in peaceful times, when there is no strike, can you cite instances where meetings have been prohibited?

MR. GOMPERS. Yes, sir.

SENATOR STERLING. Where workers could not meet and discuss their grievances and appoint committees?

MR. GOMPERS. Yes, sir; yes, sir; time without number. . . .

About the 27th or 28th of August Mr. Fitzpatrick, Mr. Davis, of the Iron and Steel Workers, Mr. Foster, secretary of the organizing committee, and myself,

with Mr. Hannon of the International Association of Machinists, by appointment, had the honor of a conference with the President, where we presented to him this entire situation and related to him the efforts which had been made to have a conference with Judge Gary and the inability to secure such a conference. The President expressed the belief that, in his judgment, a conference might be helpful to adjust the differences. We asked him whether he would not use his good offices to try to bring about a conference with Judge Gary and a committee of the employees of his corporation. We presented to him the thought that the subsidiary companies are under the general jurisdiction of the United States Steel Corporation, and that if the corporation, speaking for the corporation itself, as well as for its subsidiary companies, would have a conference with a committee representing the men in the various plants of the corporation, we would regard that as being proper. The President seemed to be in favor of our position that a conference should be held. I am not divulging any confidence. I would not do that if I was conscious of it, particularly in the case of the President, or in the case of any other man, but the President said that he would make an effort to try to bring about such a conference, and try to prevail upon Judge Gary to permit such a conference to take place.

The President, I am advised, did make such effort, and upon a telegram being sent to him asking what result had accrued from the efforts he had made, said that he was a bit discouraged, and yet would not give up trying. That is substantially his answer.

The committee having the organization of the men in charge met at the office of the American Federation of Labor. I met with them, and the entire situation was gone over.

On the following Monday—that is, I think, on September 8—I met with the committee again and advised that the strike, if possible, should be deferred. On the following day the officers of the 24 organizations, together with the committee, met, and when the reports were given, up to the minute, of the situation existing, the men—the responsible officers of the organizations involved—decided by unanimous vote to inform the men that, in compliance with their expressed will, unless a conference was held with Judge Gary and the committee in the meantime, they would be authorized to strike on September 22.

I had left Washington on the Monday preceding the Tuesday when that meeting was held. That day my father passed away and I was not in the best possible frame of mind to do anything.

On Wednesday a telegram was received from the President, addressed to me at the offices of the American Federation of Labor in Washington, asking me whether I could not intervene and endeavor to prevail upon the men to defer the strike until after the presidential industrial conference of October 6.

Over long-distance telephone I dictated a letter to my secretary, addressed to Mr. Fitzpatrick, in which the telegram of the President was quoted, and urging that the President's request be complied with and such action taken as would bring about that result. That letter was written and mailed to Mr. Fitzpatrick, addressed to him at Chicago, was it not?

MR. FITZPATRICK. No; I got it here.

MR. GOMPERS. It was handed to Mr. Fitzpatrick, who was still in Washington. A few days after that a letter was received from Mr. Fitzpatrick, speaking of the conditions which obtained; that

it was impossible to hold the men; that, even if the committee would assume the fullest authority that they had and tried to prevent the strike, the men were in such a frame of mind that they could not be prevented from striking. They would strike, whatever the course of the committee would be. . . .

THE CHAIRMAN. Now, Mr. Gompers, I want to direct your thought to this. We might just as well be perfectly frank about the situation. You have probably read a speech on the floor of the House made a few days ago concerning Mr. Foster. The papers are carrying reported statements of Mr. Foster, I do not know the dates they were purported to have been made, but signed "Yours for the I.W.W.," and "Yours for the revolution," and things of that kind, and Mr. Foster is quite a factor, apparently, in this strike. Now, it is charged and has been charged on the floors of Congress that the American Federation of Labor is not really squarely behind this strike. No one ever imputes any question about your patriotism. You did as much to win the war as anybody, and everybody knows it. But the American Federation of Labor, they say, is not squarely behind the strike, but that radicals like Foster, with views which are quoted from his books, whether they be ancient or modern, I know not, but statements made by him and reports of Mr. Duncan, who, I think, is vice president of the American Federation of Labor, is he not?

MR. GOMPERS. Yes.

THE CHAIRMAN. From the Budapest conference about Mr. Foster—

MR. GOMPERS. Yes.

THE CHAIRMAN. That that class of men, radicals, who are against the institutions of our country, are using this in a way and getting into the American

Federation of Labor and trying to control it in that way. Now, that is a pretty blunt question and a frank question, and I would like to have you discuss it.

MR. GOMPERS. In response to the question of Senator Phipps I made a very brief reference to Mr. Foster. I want to amplify that a bit.

I have heard it said, "Oh, that mine enemy would write a book." That is the sum total of the antagonism directed to Mr. Foster. He wrote a book, and when a young man dogmatically laid down the phantasies of his brain. Let me say, sir, that no one had a greater antipathy toward the personality of another than I had toward Mr. Foster. I mean, toward his attitude. I did not care how he looked or appeared, but to me a man who would assume the position that Mr. Foster took at the Zurich conference when representing the I.W.W. and claiming recognition by that conference he wanted Mr. James Duncan, a magnificent, intelligent man, a man of high type of character, excluded from the conference, was in about the same category with Mr. Haywood and others of that type.

THE CHAIRMAN. When was that conference?

MR. GOMPERS. That was about 1910, something like that, or 1911.

THE CHAIRMAN. And he appeared at that conference as the representative of the I.W.W.?

MR. GOMPERS. Yes, sir; that is, he so claimed. I have no authority for saying that he did, but he so claimed. Then Mr. Foster wrote that pamphlet.

SENATOR McKELLAR. When was that written?

MR. GOMPERS. Oh, about a year or so after. That pamphlet on "Syndicalism" carried out the thought that he presented to the Zurich International Labor Conference.

I should say, in passing, that Mr. Foster was not admitted by that international meeting but that Mr. Duncan was seated as the representative of the American Federation of Labor.

About a year after that meeting at Zurich—no, about two years after the Zurich meeting, and about a year after that pamphlet had been printed, I was at a meeting of the Chicago Federation of Labor, conducted under the presidency of Mr. John Fitzpatrick. I was called upon to make and did make an address. One of the delegates arose after I had concluded and expressed himself as being thoroughly in accord with what President Gompers had said; that it would be wise for the men in the labor movement of Chicago and of the entire country to follow the thought and the philosophy and so forth which President Gompers had enunciated in his address. I did not know who was the delegate. He was a new personality to me. I might say that I was rather flattered and pleased at the fact that there was general comment of approval of not only my utterances but of the delegate who had first spoken after I had concluded.

Much to my amazement, after the meeting was over I was informed that the delegate was W. Z. Foster, the man who had appeared in Zurich and the man who had written that pamphlet. I think I addressed a letter to him expressing my appreciation of his change of attitude, his change of mind, and pointing out to him that pursuing that constructive policy he could be of real service to the cause of labor. He was a man of ability, a man of good presence, gentle in expression, a commander of good English, and I encouraged him. I was willing to help build a golden bridge for mine enemy to pass over. I was willing to welcome an erring brother into the ranks of constructive labor. And in view of what Mr. Foster has done in helping to bring about better conditions among the stockyard workers of Chicago and of the balance of the country, in view of the lawful, honorable methods which he has pursued in this situation now under investigation, he is entitled to have something better than a mistaken past thrown not only in his teeth and in his face, but held up to the contumely of the world in order now to make his activities impossible or to neutralize them. That is the situation, Mr. Chairman.

THE CHAIRMAN. You say, then, do you, Mr. Gompers, that his views expressed by him in his book on "Syndicalism" and his views expressed at the time you speak of have changed?

MR. GOMPERS. I have no doubt, and I have no hesitancy in saying so, sir.

Now, Mr. Chairman, here is a list of the 24 organizations and the names of their executive officers which constitute the general organizing and strike committee. Mr. Foster is not an executive officer; he is not a member of that body. He has been chosen by them as secretary to perform the secretarial work . . . .

THE CHAIRMAN. I have just one more question which I would like to have in the record. If Mr. Foster had not changed his mind on these fundamental questions from the time that you speak of, I take it that you would not be willing to have him do anything with this strike situation, would you?

MR. GOMPERS. Not at all. On the contrary, as I stated in the early part of my remarks this morning, I was elected the first chairman of this conference committee in June, 1918. Mr. Foster was elected secretary. I would not have served with Mr. Foster if he had not changed his views.

Now, Mr. Chairman, I do not want to change the trend of questioning that is intended to be pursued further, but I should like to present some other matters.

May I say this, that Mr. Foster not only declared to others and to me that if any time I believed his occupancy of the secretaryship of the organizing and conference committee was inimical to the interests of the organizations or to the iron and steel workers, his resignation could be had at any minute on simple request or intimation. . . .

We must recognize this fact; the war was gloriously won; the scheme of autocracy, imperialism and militarism has been crushed; the thing and the spirit must be crushed, whether that be political, economical, or industrial, and the time has come for a new understanding of relations between employer and employee. The time has come when the workers insist on a new understanding and a new relationship not only between nations and nations but between man and man, regardless of their situation in life. No man can hold himself and say, "I am master of all I survey"; no corporation can do that in our time. . . . The workers of our country, the citizenship of our country, demand that there shall be a larger degree of fairness and justice and democracy in industry. . . .

John Fitzpatrick: TESTIMONY BEFORE THE SENATE INVESTIGATING COMMITTEE

THE CHAIRMAN. Just what is your relationship to this strike? That is what
we want to get.

MR. FITZPATRICK. Chairman of the national committee for organizing iron and
steel workers.

* * *

SENATOR JONES. . . . How did the conditions in the steel mills affect labor in
other lines?

MR. FITZPATRICK. The hours are long
and the wages are small, and the treatment—you can not describe the treatment. Other employers meet and they
discuss the situation in the steel mills,
and they want to know why they can
not do the same in their institutions,
why they can not work 12 hours, why
they can not pay a pittance for the labor
that they use, and when our organizations would go in arbitration matters or
meet employers, the barrier that was
held up before them, the thing that they
could not get over, was "Why don't you
go to the steel mills? You get the steel
mill conditions up there, get the hours
down, and the wages up there, and
when you do that, of course we will
treat with you then." And that was the
one situation that made it absolutely im-
perative that the steel mills be organized, because it held the balance of the
labor movement back.

* * *

SENATOR WOLCOTT. Boiling it down to
figures, Mr. Fitzpatrick, the situation
was this: that 98,000 men, in round numbers, voted for the strike, which involved
the employment of 500,000 men?

MR. FITZPATRICK. I think it would be
somewhat different from that, because
when men in the mills saw that there
was a situation which might bring hope
into their lives and into their homes,
50,000 men joined the organization between July and the date that we compiled the vote. Fifty thousand, so that
we have 150,000 when the vote was
compiled.

SENATOR McKELLAR. Have any joined
since; and if so, how many, if you know?

MR. FITZPATRICK. Our report yesterday was 340,000.

* * *

THE CHAIRMAN. Now this committee
wants to get all of that information. Now
can you give us information as to the
proportion of men in the mills who are
naturalized Americans or native-born
Americans and those who are aliens. Can
you give us any light on that?

MR. FITZPATRICK. No. We never go
into it in that way. We have to organize the employees of the steel mills.
Now, if those men were not employed
by the steel mills, we would not have
them in the organization. The fact that
they are in the steel mills—if they are

From *Investigation of Strike in Steel Industries, Hearings before the Committee on Education
and Labor,* United States Senate, Sixty-sixth Congress, First Session, Pursuant to S. Res. 188 and
S. Res. 202, Part 2 (Washington, Government Printing Office, 1919), pp. 7, 9–10, 15, 28–29, 32,
35–36, 41, 43, 49–50, 67, 77, 83.

good enough for Mr. Gary to use, why they are good enough to go into our organization. . . .

* * *

THE CHAIRMAN. What are the duties of the State Constabulary, if you know?

MR. FITZPATRICK. They are a strike-breaking institution. I do not know that they have any other purpose to serve. That is what they are used for now, to break this strike, terrorize the people and drive them back to work.

* * *

Now, at Duquesne, the police officials and the State Constabulary are giving the men the choice of either going back into the mills or going to jail. These men are thrown into jail when they refuse to break the strike by going back to work under the threats of the mill town officials.

THE CHAIRMAN. Are they thrown into jail without any charges being brought against them?

MR. FITZPATRICK. Yes.

THE CHAIRMAN. And without any trials?

MR. FITZPATRICK. Yes.

THE CHAIRMAN. How general is that practice?

MR. FITZPATRICK. It is very general.

* * *

SENATOR JONES. . . . In ordering the strike, did you instruct your people to confine themselves to the property of the United States Steel Corporation?

MR. FITZPATRICK. No.

SENATOR JONES. Then in what terms did you order the strike? Was it to be a general strike, or were there to be exceptions to it, and if so, what were the exceptions?

MR. FITZPATRICK. That the men in the steel industry, as we could not get any consideration, or if the Chief Executive of this Nation could not get any consideration, that then we would cease work and we feel that this is just as much an effort on the part of labor to sustain the Executive of this Nation in this instance as it was their desire and effort to sustain it in the crisis presented in the war.

SENATOR JONES. Yes.

MR. FITZPATRICK. Just as much. Here is an institution, the Steel Corporation, which sets itself up within the confines of the United States and raised an Army, armed men, and sends them on the street to terrorize the citizenship of these communities, and then when the President of the United States asks for a conference he can not secure that conference, and the men in the mills have made up their minds that that is a menace to this Nation, and they say that they are with the President of the United States, the Chief Executive of this Nation, in seeing that the chief officer of this Nation will be respected and that an institution in this country can not be bigger than the President.

THE CHAIRMAN. Do you think that part of Pennsylvania is not safe for democracy?

MR. FITZPATRICK. There is absolutely no democracy there. It is a tyranny and an autocracy, and I do not think that the equal of it ever existed in Russia.

* * *

SENATOR PHIPPS. . . . I am asking you what would be the object of the owners of the mill in requiring that their men whom they pay by the hour should work 12 hours a day instead of 8 hours?

MR. FITZPATRICK. Men who are brutalized in that way do not feel themselves as free men. They feel that they are serfs, and they take on the spirit of the serf, and they go on their way in humble submission to the authority that is above them. If they worked the 8-hour day, the spirit of Americanism would come into their lives. They would wish to surround their wives and children with better homes, better food, greater opportunity, and try to develop their children, so that they might grow into the kind of American citizens that we want to have in this country.

* * *

MR. FITZPATRICK. . . . If the members of this committee would go with our organizers without the knowledge of the public or the mill-town officials, or the guards, or the mounted police, just go into some of those places, and then see the treatment that our organizers—that is accorded the citizenship of those places—then you would have something that would open the eyes of the committee as to the dangers in America.

SENATOR WALSH. Some of us want to stay here until after we have voted on the treaty, because we might get shot.

MR. FITZPATRICK. I am very much in that condition myself, Senator. When I go into western Pennsylvania I kiss my wife and babies good-by, absolutely, because I do not ever expect to see them again.

SENATOR WALSH. It is as bad as that?

MR. FITZPATRICK. Yes, sir.

* * *

THE CHAIRMAN. Is there a good deal of what we call Bolshevism among these workers in the steel mills?

MR. FITZPATRICK. The only Bolshevist I saw over there are the mill town officials and the men who deliberately defy the Constitution of the United States. Would you call this a Bolshevist?

* * *

THE CHAIRMAN. Well, now, Mr. Fitzpatrick, there is a good deal of talk in Congress about the doctrines of Mr. Foster as have been enunciated in a book he has written, which perhaps you are familiar with, "Syndicalism."

* * *

MR. FITZPATRICK. I have looked through them; yes.

THE CHAIRMAN. Do you sympathize with some of those doctrines?

MR. FITZPATRICK. They are things that are past and gone. They have had to go into the graveyard and search around there to get something. They have not got anything on Foster, except something that has been dead and buried so long that it has no more use; and that is where they went.

* * *

SENATOR WALSH. What was his attitude toward this country during the war, if you know?

MR. FITZPATRICK. Absolutely loyal, and he did everything in his power to assist in every way. I worked with him. I worked with him during the whole of the war, and I know the service that he rendered to the country. I think that he rendered as great a service, not only to the United States Government, but to the Allies, as any man.

THE CHAIRMAN. Have you ever discussed this book with him at all?

MR. FITZPATRICK. Oh, he joked about the views that he had in his younger days, when he associated with men who were actuated with radical thoughts, and he was imbued by it, but when he got both his feet on the ground and knew how to weigh matters with better discretion and more conscience, he had forgot all those things that he learned when he was a boy, and is now doing a man's thinking in the situation.

* * *

THE CHAIRMAN. . . . If the Steel Corporation would agree to refer all difficulties to arbitration, would you be willing to do that?

MR. FITZPATRICK. Yes.

THE CHAIRMAN. And end the strike?

MR. FITZPATRICK. Yes.

THE CHAIRMAN. Would you be willing to submit them to a board to be chosen by the President of the United States?

MR. FITZPATRICK. Yes, sir.

THE CHAIRMAN. So that you are willing to end the strike in that way?

MR. FITZPATRICK. Yes, sir.

THE CHAIRMAN. Do you say now if the steel people will do that, that you will call the strike off?

MR. FITZPATRICK. I have not the authority to call the strike off, Mr. Chairman.

THE CHAIRMAN. But you feel that it could be called off?

MR. FITZPATRICK. My knowledge of the men who are handling the situation makes me believe that they would be glad to meet the situation in that way.

PUBLIC OPINION AND THE STEEL STRIKE

THE ADVERTISING CAMPAIGN

ON September 27, the fifth day of the strike, an advertising campaign was begun to induce the striking steel workers to abandon their protest. While the advertisements were apparently intended for the strikers themselves, they had, unquestionably, by reason of their prominence, an important influence in forming public opinion on the causes and issues of the strike. Between September 27 and October 8 over thirty full-page advertisements denouncing the leadership of the strike and calculated to undermine the morale of the strikers, appeared in the various Pittsburgh newspapers. They were printed in English and generally in four or five foreign languages as well. In sum, the purport of these advertisements was that it was *un-American* for the steel workers to be on strike.

These advertisements, obviously prepared by competent professional skill, were carefully designed and were characterized by an effective display. A number of them contained a half-page cartoon of "Uncle Sam," garbed in stars and stripes, with his hand to his mouth calling in the direction of steel mills pictured in the background: "Go back to work!" This exhortation was printed in eight languages. The page-wide streamer line in heavy black type at the top read: "America is calling you." The line at the bottom read: "Go back to work!" ...

The full-page advertisements as carried by the *Leader* on October 5 and 6 and by the *Chronicle-Telegraph* on October 6, exhibited in heavy type in the body of the advertisement the following statements:

The steel strike can't win. It is uncalled for and un-American. It is led by men who apparently are trying to establish the "red" rule of anarchy and bolshevism in this land of opportunity and liberty. The American institution of majority rule is threatened by a malicious, radical group of agitators. They are trying to throw hundreds of thousands of wellpaid, prosperous workmen out of employment because of the whims of a very small minority.

Don't be fooled any longer. Stand by America and all that America means. Stick to your job and keep up "good times."

"GO BACK TO WORK"

On Saturday, September 27, the *Chronicle-Telegraph* carried a page advertisement with a slogan three times repeated across the full width of the page in large type: "GO BACK TO WORK MONDAY." Besides quotations from the booklet "Syndicalism" by W. Z. Foster, the advertisement displayed such statements as these:

Yesterday the enemy of liberty was Prussianism. Today it is radicalism.

Masquerading under the cloak of the American Federation of Labor a few Radicals are striving for power. They hope to seize control of the industries and to turn the company over to the "red" rule of Syndicalism.

Among the slogans presented in the advertising campaign were the following, printed in type an inch to two inches high:

From The Interchurch World Movement, *Report on the Steel Strike of 1919.* Copyright, 1920, by Harcourt, Brace & World, Inc.

AMERICA IS CALLING YOU
THE STEEL STRIKE WILL FAIL, BE A
100% AMERICAN, STAND BY AMERICA.

THE STEEL STRIKE CAN'T WIN,
BOYS! LET'S BE 100% AMERICANS
NOW, EUROPE'S NOT WHAT IT USED
TO BE, MAYBE THE DOORS OF THE
OLD U.S.A. WILL NOT AGAIN OPEN
TO THEM IF FOREIGN BORN NOW
HERE RETURN TO EUROPE AND
WANT TO COME BACK.

Almost invariably with others appeared
the slogan, "GO BACK TO WORK."
This was varied by the slogan which
appeared on Saturday, "GO BACK TO
WORK MONDAY." . . .

The representations in the following
advertisement are a fair sample of those
to be found in all. That they are
misrepresentations will be seen by comparison with the Main Report of the
Commission. The English part of the
advertisement (half the page was given
to translations into seven foreign languages) is quoted in full:

The Steel Strike Can't Win

Here are ten reasons why the strike will
fail: ten reasons why you and every other
man who is loyal to America will go back to
work:

1. There is no good American reason for
the strike.

2. A very large majority of the workers
did not want to strike.

3. The strike is not between workers and
employers, but between revolutionists and
America.

4. It is becoming more and more apparent that the strike is merely the diabolical
attempt of a few Radicals to seize industry
and plant Bolshevism in this country.

5. The strike is doomed to fail, just as all
unpopular and unpatriotic movements have
failed in this country.

6. Public sentiment is against the strike;
Americans have great sympathy for genuine
wrongs but they have neither sympathy nor
tolerance for Radicals who seek to use organized labor as a tool in their nefarious
campaigns against industry and American
liberty.

7. The strike is an economic failure and
the loss will be felt by everyone including
you.

8. America will never stand for the "red"
rule of Bolshevism, I.W.W.ism or any other
"ism" that seeks to tear down the Constitution. Radicalism must be put down.

9. There is a strong possibility that the
Huns had a hand in fomenting the strike,
hoping to retard industrial progress in America.

10. Keep America busy and prosperity
will continue. . . .

LETTER OF REVEREND THOMAS DEVLIN

TO the Editor of the [Pittsburgh]
Chronicle-Telegraph.

Dear Sir: For more than 36 years I
have lived among the iron and steel
workers of this great city. I believe that
no one even of my colleagues has been in
closer touch with the men of muscle and
brawn who have contributed so much to

the building up of our Nation. My home
is in the shadows of a forest of smoke-
stacks of the largest steel mill in Pittsburgh. The whirr of machinery, the
rumbling of the trains, the noise and din
of ceaseless industry sound in my ears
day and night. Two generations of working men whom I have served in the most

From *Investigation of Strike in Steel Industries, Hearings before the Committee on Education
and Labor*, United States Senate, Sixty-sixth Congress, First Session, Pursuant to S. Res. 188 and
S. Res 202, Part 2 (Washington, Government Printing Office, 1919), pp. 901–902.

intimate relationship will testify to my interest in and devotion to the working man. For him I have sacrificed health, pleasure, comfort, preferment. No one, therefore, can suspect me of any lack of sympathy with, or unfriendliness toward, Nature's nobleman, the honest toiler of the Nation, when I criticize the motives and methods of those who are conducting the movement for the organization of the iron and steel workers. I admit that there are many things in the conditions of the industrial, economic, and social life of the workers which call loudly for betterment. To-day when the world is being reconstructed the need of social justice is recognized more and more by the enlightened public. The desired improvement will not be obtained, however, by promoting ill-feeling and discontent, or through strikes or class warfare. The President of the United States has suggested the proper method for the settlement of the differences which have occasioned the present strike. He has called a conference of representative employers and employees in which all questions in dispute will be considered calmly and reasonably.

The American Federation of Labor, however, seems to have fallen into the hands of the Bolsheviki and the Reds. It has refused to listen to the appeal of President Wilson to await the result of the conference. It has turned a deaf ear to the request of its own superior officer to comply with the President's wish, and has appointed a professed syndicalist, William Z. Foster, a vice president of the American Federation of Labor, to organize the steel workers in the great Pittsburgh district.

William Z. Foster has written a book in which he describes himself and his fellow syndicalists as unscrupulous in their choice of weapons to fight their battles with capitalism. They allow no consideration of legality, religion, patriotism, honor, duty, or anything else to stand in the way of adoption of effective tactics. The only sentiment they know is loyalty as they see it to the interests of the working classes. They are in utter revolt against capitalism in all its phases. The syndicalist movement, Foster says, is a union-labor movement which intends to overthrow capitalism and disorganize society. This movement sees in the State only an instrument of oppression and a bungling administration of industry, and proposes to exclude it from future society. It sees no need for any general supervising governmental body. To accomplish its purposes it proposes to disorganize the police and military forces, or so weaken them as to render them inefficient. It will make use of sabotage and every method, whether underhand or unmanly. No consideration of what is just, fair, or civilized will restrain it. Its principle is—the end justifies the means.

The Kaiser, Hindenburg or Von Tirpitz have nothing on Foster. He is in the class of Trotsky, Lenin, and the Bolsheviki.

This, then, is the man who has been appointed by the American Federation of Labor to organize the honest, hard-working men of Pittsburgh and to promote a strike during the period of the world's economic readjustment.

Why do not our sensible sons of toil resent the insult offered them by the appointment of a syndicalist to direct them?

Why do not the civil authorities arrest and imprison a professed anarchist worse in his teachings than Bergman, Goldman, or any of the Russian Reds?

As for the men of Holy Cross, I have every confidence in their intelligence and good judgment and have no fear that they will be influenced by the sophistries of the radicals, but as a matter of precaution I have given warning that if any should follow the leadership of Foster it would be equivalent to indorsing his doctrines and I should regard them as apostates from the Catholic faith, traitors to their country, and enemies to authority.

THOMAS DEVLIN,
Pastor of Holy Cross Church,
Pittsburgh, Pa.

TESTIMONY OF RESIDENTS OF MILL TOWNS

MR. J. S. OURSLER, GENERAL MANAGER OF THE HOMESTEAD STEEL WORKS

THE CHAIRMAN. Your name is J. S. Oursler, and you are general manager of the Homestead Steel Works?

MR. OURSLER. Yes, sir!

THE CHAIRMAN. And what is the total number of employees here?

MR. OURSLER. The total number of employees is 11,500.

THE CHAIRMAN. And how many out of that total are now at work?

MR. OURSLER. Nine thousand and forty-four.

＊ ＊ ＊

THE CHAIRMAN. What percentage of the number employed are foreigners?

MR. OURSLER. We have 40 per cent Americans, 9 per cent colored.

THE CHAIRMAN. And do you call the colored men Americans?

MR. OURSLER. Yes.

SENATOR MCKELLAR. And of the 25 per cent of your employees who are on strike, what percentage of them are foreigners, would you say? . . .

MR. OURSLER. Ninety-nine and nine-tenths per cent are foreigners who are out on strike.

＊ ＊ ＊

THE CHAIRMAN. Have you had any violence from these people who are out on strike, Mr. Oursler? Has there been any violence at all?

MR. OURSLER. I should say yes; we had a number of individual cases where a man was beaten up and of throwing bricks through a window, but we have not had any serious amount of violence.

＊ ＊ ＊

SENATOR PHIPPS. Is there any definite organized effort at the present time to keep the men away from the plant?

MR. OURSLER. No; not a great deal of it; just here and there is all. They did have the plants pretty well picketed, but that is practically over with and there is very little picketing to-day.

SENATOR MCKELLAR. Do you allow them to hold their meetings?

MR. OURSLER. Yes, sir.

SENATOR MCKELLAR. Is there any curbing of their speech at all at those meetings?

MR. OURSLER. They have to speak in English; that is all.

＊ ＊ ＊

SENATOR MCKELLAR. Is there any complaint on account of the wages on the part of those who are out?

MR. OURSLER. No.

＊ ＊ ＊

THE CHAIRMAN. You say that you have a good many Russians, have you?

MR. OURSLER. Yes, sir; we have 628 Russians.

＊ ＊ ＊

THE CHAIRMAN. And do you notice

From *Investigation of Strike in Steel Industries, Hearings before the Committee on Education and Labor,* United States Senate, Sixty-sixth Congress, First Session, Pursuant to S. Res. 188 and S. Res. 202, Part 2 (Washington, Government Printing Office, 1919), pp. 477–479, 481–482.

that they have a tendency toward Bolshevism themselves?

MR. OURSLER. Yes, sir.

* * *

SENATOR STERLING. What proportion of those who are out on strike—of the 25 per cent of the employees now out on strike—are Slovak, do you suppose?

MR. OURSLER. I think that possibly all of the Slovak are out on strike, and that this strike is a Slovak strike. I classify the Americans—any man that has taken out naturalization papers is classified as an American.

* * *

THE CHAIRMAN. Why did they go out? How did they come to go out?

MR. OURSLER. I think perhaps the best way that I can answer that question is to repeat a conversation which occurred between one of our superintendents and one of his men. He met him and he said to him "What are you striking for?" The man answered, "I am striking for a dollar an hour, eight hours work, no bosses, no superintendents."

The superintendent said to him "Well, you earn $15 or $16 a day. Is that not enough?" The answer was, "Oh, yes; but I want no bosses; get on the street car, no buy a ticket—union car. Get on the railroad, no buy ticket—union car."

"But, Joe," he was asked, "do you want the man who works around the shop, the laborer, to get a dollar an hour?" "Jesus Christ, no," he said.

* * *

SENATOR STERLING. Now, Mr. Oursler, you have the basic eight-hour day for all, have you not? That is, you pay time and a half for overtime; that is true, is it not?

MR. OURSLER. Yes, sir.

* * *

THE CHAIRMAN. Now, is what they want not to be permitted to get any overtime?

MR. OURSLER. They want 8 hours a day and 11 hours' pay for it.

REVEREND ADELBERT KAZINCY

MR. RUBIN. Reverend, you are a Roman Catholic priest, are you?

FATHER KAZINCY. Yes, sir.

MR. RUBIN. And duly ordained?

FATHER KAZINCY. Yes, sir.

SENATOR MCKELLAR. I beg your pardon, Father. Had I known that you were a priest we certainly would have dispensed with the oath.

FATHER KAZINCY. That is all right.

MR. RUBIN. What church and where?

FATHER KAZINCY. St Michael's Catholic Church, in Braddock. . . . Well, on the 10th of September we had a mission, so called, or, as others understand it, a revival, in our church. On the 14th of September, the following day, which was Monday, the men were leaving church at 10 o'clock in the morning, filing out of the church nicely and peaceably, no doubt with very sanitary thoughts in their minds, and they were suddenly attacked by two of the State constabulary on the steps of the church, all of which I have sent an explanation in the form of a telegram to the governor of the State—

MR. RUBIN. Don't you mean on the 21st?

FATHER KAZINCY. On the 21st. I per-

Ibid., pp. 542–546.

sonally walked out in the middle of the street, leaving the church, to stop these men and ask them what did they mean by clubbing peaceful worshippers leaving the church. They said they had orders that these men must move on. I said, "You do not expect them to grow wings in two minutes or in a half an hour. They have been listening to a sermon in the church. They are not a lot of birds, and they can not fly away." They said, "We do not do anything except to keep them on the move."

I said, "They are moving nicely and quietly." They turned around and left.

* * *

MR. RUBIN. How about the number of times that the persons have omitted to go to church?

FATHER KAZINCY. Well, these are from the furnaces in the Braddock mills; and in those furnaces they allow the men to go to church every second Sunday. There are nine furnaces there, and furnaces H and A allow the men to go to church every second Sunday. The balance of the nine furnaces do not allow their men at all to go to church. Some get a Sunday off, perhaps, once in six months; but it is not taking care of their souls. . . .

THE CHAIRMAN. Have you noticed, in coming into contact with these men, any hostility upon their part toward the institutions of this country?

FATHER KAZINCY. Absolutely none. They have been branded as anarchists and Bolshevists, and they resent it.

SENATOR McKELLAR. Do you know whether there are any among them?

FATHER KAZINCY. No, they are Catholics, you know, and Catholics can not afford to do that unless they give up their religion. . . .

THE CHAIRMAN. You started to tell us about the conditions there.

FATHER KAZINCY. The men are worked from 10 to 13 hours a day. You gentlemen will find that out if you will go to Braddock, and if you will accept me I will act as cicerone for you out there. The conditions under which they are living are bad for America. The housing conditions are terrible. The work conditions, the hours of work, are absolutely impossible, and I think that it tends to make the men become disgusted with the country, and they will say, "Well, let us go back to the old country; perhaps it is going to be better than it is for us here." There is no hope of them bettering their condition, for they work from the time the whistle begins to blow in the morning until they are whistled out at 6 o'clock in the morning [sic] they must be at the gates there, and they have to work all the time. For instance, Mr. Gary has been quoted as saying that there are many millions of dollars put in the savings account. I would like to see him show us that money. It is the business class, the people in Johnstown and others. He says that he desires to have them have checking accounts. They do not have checking accounts. They do not believe in checking accounts. When they save a little money, they have the children, and they raise their children on bread and coffee, and they have to sustain themselves and their wives, and they have to be satisfied with their life.

THE CHAIRMAN. You say that the living conditions are terrible. That is a conclusion. Let us know what you mean by that.

FATHER KAZINCY. The housing conditions, the hours of work, and the wage for the work, and the amount of the work.

SENATOR STERLING. Now, about the housing conditions, will you describe those?

FATHER KAZINCY. Well, two rooms, as a rule, are the headquarters of the workers. The lower part is a kitchen and upstairs is the living room, if you can call it such, and the sleeping room for the family, and they have to sleep there. Sometimes they have boarders and sometimes there are four or five sleeping in a room.

SENATOR STERLING. As a matter of fact, do many of them have less than four rooms?

FATHER KAZINCY. Yes; most of them have only two rooms. . . .

MR. T. J. DAVIES, OF NEW CASTLE, PA.

THE CHAIRMAN. State to the reporter your name, address, and business.

MR. DAVIES. My name is T. J. Davies, New Castle, Pa., the Shenango Works, and, incidentally, Newcastle Works, two tin-mills, representing 5,000 tin-mill workers.

THE CHAIRMAN. You say you represent 5,000 tin-mill workers?

MR. DAVIES. Five thousand tin-mill workers. I am engaged in one plant where they employ 3,200 tin workers. . . .

THE CHAIRMAN. You represent, then, what you believe to be the opinion of the men, but there has been no action taken?

MR. DAVIES. No, sir. . . .

MR. DAVIES. . . . We went to the main entrance, one of the men working with me; we are nine on the crew, and we arranged to go together, and he drove the car, his own car, and we passed the main entrance, and there was a very large mob standing on the outside of the main entrance, but we passed through it; we did not turn into the mill there; we turned in at the lower entrance and come in the block just as a great big crowd blocked our pathway, or got in front of the machine, and one of them got on the dashboard, and one of my crew says to the other, he says, "Throw her into second and shoot the gas on and let her run." And she did and we got in. We got into the mill and we were determined to shoot our way in and to shoot our way out if necessary.

SENATOR STERLING. On what date was that?

MR. DAVIES. September 22.

THE CHAIRMAN. How many men had gone out of the mill then?

MR. DAVIES. Well, on the first day I judge we would have been about 1,000 short out of the 3,200 . . . .

THE CHAIRMAN. About how many are out now?

MR. DAVIES. There are now out, I suppose, about—I would guess, about 500. We are under a state of practical military law. The returned soldiers took hold after some of the mob violence, some of the returned soldiers volunteered to protect the place, and then the board of trade held a citizens' meeting, and 186 members of the board of trade, and leading citizens, stood up and took oath at one time under the sheriff of the county, in one meeting. We were afraid for the homes and the institutions of the city, judging by the violence that had occurred on the Monday.

SENATOR STERLING. When you say they took the oath, you mean they were sworn in as deputies?

MR. DAVIES. Sworn in as deputies, yes, sir. There are about 700 deputies, and the place is practically, as far as deputies can make it, under military law; and while we have not removed the terror-

Ibid., pp. 439-441, 444-452.

ism from around the homes where the different foreigners live, they are kind of colonized around there, different colonies.

THE CHAIRMAN. What proportion of these men were what you term foreigners that went out?

MR. DAVIES. The proportion of foreigners would be out of the 1,000, I would say about 99 per cent, or better. . . .

SENATOR PHIPPS. You referred to violence which, I think, from your statement, occurred about the time of the walkout?

MR. DAVIES. Yes, sir; it occurred on the first turn.

SENATOR PHIPPS. Of what did that consist; what was the extent of the violence?

MR. DAVIES. In one case they just picked up a Ford machine and turned it right around and the whole crew had to start the other way. There was about 1,000 of them and they increased from the first to the second and third turns. The first turn they didn't stop us; we got in.

SENATOR PHIPPS. They tried to stop you?

MR. DAVIES. They tried to stop the machine; if we had stopped once it would not have moved again; we kept going. That was the first turn. When they found out there were 15 mills out of 30 running they became aggravated and increased in number on the following turn; and on the following turn members of my family passed in. They stopped them going in. They stopped some of my crew going in on the first turn—one man—and he turned back on account of his wife; he got scared. On the second turn they increased in number. They had three Americans. I seen the crowd and they had 3 Americans out of about 500.

They increased, and on the third turn they became bolder. They whipped the city police; they whipped the county police; they stabbed one of the policemen, and they stabbed the other—and three of our men they took into the crowd and beat up mercilessly. My brother came out of the mill and they tried to stop that machine, but they got away somehow.

There was about 1,000 people there. They have beat these men and beat the police and whipped the county police and these others, and when there became such a large crowd, about 40 returned soldiers volunteered to be deputy sheriffs and were deputized. They found some bayonets and fixed their bayonets on their guns and started in on duty to scatter the mobs of foreigners that were everywhere around the mills.

THE CHAIRMAN. What town was that?

MR. DAVIES. Newcastle. . . .

SENATOR PHIPPS. How long have you been in this country?

MR. DAVIES. Twenty-four years.

SENATOR PHIPPS. I assume you are an American citizen now; are you?

MR. DAVIES. Yes, sir. . . .

SENATOR PHIPPS. About what are your average earnings? . . .

MR. DAVIES. I average $17 a day. The lowest paid man on my crew makes $7.50, and he is a Greek. . . . I have been away 15 months in France and just returned eight weeks ago. They have received, I think, two advances.

SENATOR PHIPPS. What was your mission in France? . . .

MR. DAVIES. I was a Y.M.C.A. worker. . . .

SENATOR STERLING. Are there any union men in your immediate crew?

MR. DAVIES. In the next crew to me, the president was in the crew, and I used to have talks with him, and I tried to get him to tell me what was doing, like the most of us were doing. We wanted to know what was doing.

SENATOR STERLING. That was in a perfectly friendly way?

MR. DAVIES. Yes; and he took it in good part. He never asked us to join. We got along there friendly with them.

SENATOR STERLING. You say that in the next crew to you was a union man who was president of the union?

MR. DAVIES. Yes, sir.

SENATOR STERLING. Of what union?

MR. DAVIES. Of the Amalgamated Association. . . .

SENATOR PHIPPS. Now, from time to time, as little differences have arisen in the mills, questions of working conditions or any complaints that might arise, have those complaints been put up to the foremen, the superintendent, or to you?

MR. DAVIES. Why, the humblest man in the mill, foreign or American, does not have to accept finally anything from them. Any grievance he may want to make he can make to the foreman, and if the foreman won't take it up, he can just simply open the door of the main office and walk right in to the superintendent. That condition obtains, to the best of my knowledge and belief—to my knowledge, all through the operations of the company. If grievances are felt, the humblest man in the mill can walk past the foreman right to the general superintendent and get things remedied very quickly.

SENATOR PHIPPS. Do you know of any instances where committees have been appointed to present these grievances to the superintendent?

MR. DAVIES. I have never known of the necessity. Each man, all of us, can go off-handedly, if we like, to the superintendent. We do not have to stop at the foreman. We can take it to the manager. Things that they want remedied. For instance we had a complaint which was a big one, and it was taken to the assistant superintendent. It was a rougher's question.

SENATOR STERLING. What?

MR. DAVIES. A rougher's question. The roughers were asked to do something. They were asked to lift bars and put them in a place which was supposed to be of advantage to the company, and the foreman said, "You have got to lift them." Some of the boys told him it was not necessary, and they took their complaint to the manager. He said it would be immediately attended to and it was changed. That was a pretty good-sized committee. I suppose there were about 25 or 30, and that is a good-sized committee. They went in there to the manager and took their case up, and they didn't have to do the extra lifting, the extra carrying of the bars from here to there. It was only a matter of about 18 inches of lift which they saved by making the complaint to the superintendent, but it was listened to and attended to. . . .

THE CHAIRMAN. And how long do you work a day?

MR. DAVIES. I suppose seven hours. I work eight hours, you understand, but we work half in and half out. It is very strenuous work, and if you could see us at the end of a turn, we look the part. Our eyes are sunken. We work eight hours, understand.

THE CHAIRMAN. What is your compensation?

MR. DAVIES. $17 a day, about.

THE CHAIRMAN. How many days a week do you work?

MR. DAVIES. Five.

THE CHAIRMAN. Did men formerly do the same work as you do seven days a week?

MR. DAVIES. Nobody works more than I do.

THE CHAIRMAN. They could not do it?

MR. DAVIES. They could not do it. They could not work six days a week and keep it up long at our rate. We work the extra day every third week, and at the end of that we are like a rocket, about blowed up.

THE CHAIRMAN. It is pretty hard work?

MR. DAVIES. There are very few of our men at the end of a turn that do not go home with their eyes sunken, the heat and then the tremendous pace we go. There is the hard work and the heat we have to stand and the watchfulness of the work.

THE CHAIRMAN. How many years have you stood that kind of work?

MR. DAVIES. I have been at it—I have been rolling 18 years. I have been in the mills 34.

THE CHAIRMAN. You are not a member of the union?

MR. DAVIES. No, sir! not for 10 years. I was for 14.

THE CHAIRMAN. How many years were you a member of the union?

MR. DAVIES. I was a member of the Amalgamated Association for 14 years. . . .

SENATOR PHIPPS. What are their reasons for wanting to stay out of the union?

MR. DAVIES. Well, leaving well enough alone, it seems like, in general principles. The Amalgamated Association, in our estimation, has been a spent force since 1901, and the American Federation of Labor are not offering us anything. They are only holding things for combined labor. The only association that has anything to offer us, or presumes to have, is the Amalgamated Association. . . .

SENATOR PHIPPS. Is the union man in danger of being called out on a sympathy strike?

MR. DAVIES. The union man is in danger of being called out at the notion of any agitator who wants to go and rush anything in of his own notion at any particular time, and if a spirit of Bolshevism pervades the country, as there does at the present time, and he wants to call the people out on strike, he can do so, and they can resort to mob violence, and the labor unions will espouse a cause of that kind.

THE CHAIRMAN. Have you seen any indication of Bolshevism?

MR. DAVIES. Yes, sir, I have.

THE CHAIRMAN. Tell us about that.

MR. DAVIES. That is conducted like a conspiracy. That is the beginning of it. And I told you that some of these poor, misguided foreigners told me that they did not need any bosses in the mills, that the committee could run the mills.

THE CHAIRMAN. That is, their committee?

MR. DAVIES. Our committees after we were organized, and then I told you that the weapons used were terrorism, intimidation, threats to kill and threats to burn, and mob violence on the outside to stop the Americans from going in there, and they were not even naturalized. I tell you that that is labor Bolshevism. . . .

THE CHAIRMAN. What I am getting at is this. I am interested in this Americanization question just as much as this strike question. Don't you think there is some responsibility upon the mills and the employers of this country, steel and all, take them all in, not to employ men just to get their labor, when these men are opposed to the institutions of this country?

MR. DAVIES. Positively, and the Government should join with them and even put them out of the country and shoot them, if necessary. . . . To-day it is the rabid element that has captured the leaders, and then the leaders in turn are fed that inflamed spirit in the revolution that we are in at the present time. . . .

THE CHAIRMAN. I asked you the question if you considered Mr. Gompers one of the radical leaders, and your answer was that he was trying to hold his job. Don't you think that was rather unkind?

MR. DAVIES. I did not mean to be unkind, but Mr. Gompers has to adhere to the opinion of the leaders if the leaders decide upon a certain course, whether it has a Bolshevik tendency or not. Is that a fair answer?

THE CHAIRMAN. And you say that the radical leaders are trying to get possession of the American Federation of Labor?

MR. DAVIES. They have and failed. They have before and failed.

THE CHAIRMAN. And do you think that is an issue in this investigation?

MR. DAVIES. Yes, sir.

THE CHAIRMAN. And would you consider Mr. Gompers a radical leader? I suppose that you consider Mr. Foster one of the radical leaders? Would you consider Mr. Gompers a radical leader?

MR. DAVIES. Well, from that standpoint, Mr. Gompers is not a radical leader. . . .

THE CHAIRMAN. And did you have anything to do with the strike of 1901?

MR. DAVIES. Yes, sir.

THE CHAIRMAN. What was your part in that strike?

MR. DAVIES. I was national deputy vice president.

THE CHAIRMAN. And did you have some active participation in that strike?

MR. DAVIES. Yes, sir.

THE CHAIRMAN. And what did the men strike for?

MR. DAVIES. They struck to unionize all the mills.

THE CHAIRMAN. You supported that strike, you say?

MR. DAVIES. Yes, sir.

THE CHAIRMAN. And since then you have changed your mind?

MR. DAVIES. Yes, sir.

MATT O'REILLY

THE CHAIRMAN. Give your name to the reporter.

MR. O'REILLY. Matt O'Reilly. . . .

THE CHAIRMAN. Whose steel plant is it?

MR. O'REILLY. It is the steel plant of the American Steel & Wire Co. . . .

THE CHAIRMAN. . . . Are you working in the steel mill there?

MR. O'REILLY. Yes, sir; I am an assistant roller in the rod department.

THE CHAIRMAN. How long have you been there?

MR. O'REILLY. Fourteen years.

THE CHAIRMAN. And are you an American citizen?

MR. O'REILLY. I am an American citizen. . . .

THE CHAIRMAN. During the time you worked there, tell us something about the wages.

MR. O'REILLY. Well, our grievance today is not so much about the wages, as it is the working conditions and the hours and the right of free speech.

THE CHAIRMAN. Did you go out on the strike?

MR. O'REILLY. Yes.

THE CHAIRMAN. How many men are employed in that mill?

Ibid., pp. 672, 673, 674.

Mr. O'Reilly. Between 4,000 to 4,500.

The Chairman. And how many are there out on the strike?

Mr. O'Reilly. Well, I should judge there are about 4,200 out on the strike.

The Chairman. Can you tell us anything about the proportion of foreigners who are out on the strike?

Mr. O'Reilly. Well, in our town, I would say they are about 85 per cent foreigners. . . .

The Chairman. When you went out on this strike, what were you earning at the time you went out on the strike?

Mr. O'Reilly. Well, my average would run about $16 a day.

The Chairman. It would run about $16 a day? . . . why did you strike?

Mr. O'Reilly. Well, my hours are too long and we want better conditions.

The Chairman. What hours do you work?

Mr. O'Reilly. Well, I work from 6 to 6, 12 hours.

The Chairman. Twelve hours, and how many days in the week?

Mr. O'Reilly. Six days.

The Chairman. You only work six days?

Mr. O'Reilly. We do not operate on Sunday.

The Chairman. Your complaint is, then, that the hours are too long?

Mr. O'Reilly. My complaint is long hours.

The Chairman. Anything else?

Mr. O'Reilly. That is one complaint that we have, and also the working conditions.

The Chairman. Are you satisfied with the rate of wages you are receiving?

Mr. O'Reilly. Yes; I was truly satisfied with the same rate of wages.

The Chairman. That is nearly as much as a United States Senator gets.

Mr. O'Reilly. Well, but I work longer.

The Chairman. I doubt that. Maybe you work harder. What about the complaints? What complaints have you had? Have you any fault to find with getting the complaints to those officers above you?

Mr. O'Reilly. Well, Mr. Chairman, we can not get any complaint past our foreman. If we have any grievance and take it to the foreman, that is as far as we can go. If we go to the general superintendent, he calls the foreman in, and he will make it so uncomfortable for us in there that we will have to quit. . . .

JOHN J. MARTIN, MACHINIST, OHIO MILL, YOUNGSTOWN, OHIO

The Chairman. What is your name?

Mr. Martin. John J. Martin.

The Chairman. Where do you live?

Mr. Martin. Youngstown, Ohio.

The Chairman. What mill are you connected with?

Mr. Martin. The Ohio works.

The Chairman. Is that mill closed now?

Mr. Martin. Yes, sir. . . .

The Chairman. And these mills are manned by foreigners to the extent of 70 per cent?

Mr. Martin. Yes, sir. . . .

Senator McKellar. And what is your pay?

Mr. Martin. I make about $9 a day— $8.96, to be exact.

Senator Phipps. For how many hours work?

Ibid., pp. 306–309, 311–315, 317–318, 320, 322–323.

MR. MARTIN. Ten hours work; we work 10 and get 11; we work on an 8-hour basis.

THE CHAIRMAN. And how many hours do the unskilled laborers work in that mill?

MR. MARTIN. The unskilled laborers work 12 hours.

THE CHAIRMAN. And what pay do they receive?

MR. MARTIN. The lowest pay, I believe, at our plant is 42 cents an hour, and from that up. A very few, I understand—this is from hearsay—a very few receive 42 cents an hour; they most all receive more than 42 cents an hour and up as high as 50 cents an hour. . . .

SENATOR McKELLAR. And you think that only about 15 percent of the original number of 8,000 men are at work now?

MR. MARTIN. Yes, sir. There is one point that I would like to emphasize in my testimony, and it is that question of intimidation, because it has to do with our Americanism. I believe that we ought to be entitled to all the lawful rights that are coming to us, and these men have carried on a system of intimidation that has been thoroughly un-American by the massing of thousands of men at the gate and by the threatening of the burning down of homes and the killing of families.

THE CHAIRMAN. You say that they have threatened to do that?

MR. MARTIN. Yes, sir; I have been threatened myself. . . .

THE CHAIRMAN. If conditions were so favorable there, how do you account for 85 per cent of the men going out?

MR. MARTIN. I account for it by the un-American methods used by the organizers. . . .

SENATOR PHIPPS. How long have you been in Youngstown at this plant?

MR. MARTIN. I have been at Youngstown 14 years.

SENATOR PHIPPS. And during that time have there been any complaints which workmen, or committees of workmen, sought to have corrected by the foremen or superintendent of the plant?

MR. MARTIN. We have standing instructions—not standing instructions, but we have a standing invitation at all times from Mr. Gross, our manager. The way we got that was in his address to the men during our Liberty bond campaigns, etc., where he had occasion to appear before the men; he said that at any time the men had anything to say to him, be sure to come and tell him about it, any grievance. That has always been his attitude, so far as the Youngstown district is concerned. . . .

SENATOR JONES of New Mexico. Has there been any attempt by officials of the mill to prevent their joining the union?

MR. MARTIN. No, sir. . . .

SENATOR McKELLAR. Your wages are fair?

MR. MARTIN. Yes, sir.

SENATOR McKELLAR. Do most of you own your homes?

MR. MARTIN. Yes, it is a good town for people owning their homes. . . .

SENATOR McKELLAR. And there has been no complaint in regard to pay or in regard to working hours?

MR. MARTIN. No, sir; I never heard any—that is, just recent to this trouble. . . .

SENATOR McKELLAR. There was a statement made here the other day that made an impression on me, that every two weeks there were certain men, I believe rollers, I am not sure, I cannot give the technical description, but that every two weeks they had to work one class of men 24 hours at a stretch.

MR. MARTIN. Yes, that is so at our place. . . .

SENATOR MCKELLAR. How many of those men are there that work the 24 hours every two weeks of the 8,000?

MR. MARTIN. I would not think there would be over 400 or 500.

SENATOR MCKELLAR. Is there no way to avoid that very remarkable situation of a man working 24 hours?

MR. MARTIN. Well, you could avoid it if you could get the consent of the men, but I do not think the men would consent to it.

SENATOR MCKELLAR. Do they get time and a half for each hour overtime?

MR. MARTIN. All over eight hours, yes.

SENATOR MCKELLAR. Then he is resting up all the next day, he can sleep.

MR. MARTIN. He can sleep all the next day and come out that night; he changes shifts. . . .

THE CHAIRMAN. We hear a good deal about the strike being brought about by foreigners; that is one of the things we are looking into. Now, it seems a large proportion of the men employed, at least as far as the concern you are connected with is concerned, are foreigners, so we have the situation of the present steel company employing these foreigners in large numbers, more than Americans, then the foreigners bringing on the strike.

MR. MARTIN. The reason the foreigners brought the strike on, Senator, was because they were the only people asked into the organization.

THE CHAIRMAN. Were not Americans asked to join the organization?

MR. MARTIN. I have yet to meet the first American that has been approached by these organizers. . . .

SENATOR MCKELLAR. You say someone has gone ahead and scuttled the American Federation of Labor?

MR. MARTIN. Yes.

SENATOR MCKELLAR. Who was it that did it, in your judgment?

MR. MARTIN. I think, if I were to pick out the king bee I would pick out Mr. Fitzpatrick. He is ably seconded by Mr. Foster. I think that those fellows are rearing a band of buccaneers in this country that are going to upset this Government if they are not stopped. . . .

SENATOR JONES. You spoke of this book by Mr. Foster. When did you get that book?

MR. MARTIN. About six weeks ago.

SENATOR JONES. Where did you get it?

MR. MARTIN. I got it from a fellow workman. . . .

SENATOR JONES. What was your object in reading that book about three weeks ago?

MR. MARTIN. Well, I read the book to find out what position Mr. Foster took on this question, that is, this question of economics.

SENATOR JONES. Do you understand that that book is the basis of his present activity?

MR. MARTIN. Well, if you take the method being employed and the way the strike is being conducted, after reading the book they look very similar. It looks like a movement toward that end that he preaches in the book. That is my judgment.

SENATOR JONES. Has Mr. Foster or any other representative of the American Federation of Labor been preaching the doctrine of that book in your community?

MR. MARTIN. No, sir. I have never heard any official of the American Federation of Labor or any organizer preach anything like what is in that book. They always preach conciliation and cooperation between employer and employees, and there has been no idea of conciliation shown in this strike whatever. It must be rule or ruin. . . .

SENATOR WALSH. There isn't any racial feeling, is there?

MR. MARTIN. Oh, no. . . .

SENATOR McKELLAR. The great majority of those foreigners did not go into the war at all, did they?

MR. MARTIN. Oh, yes, they went.

SENATOR McKELLAR. Do you think they ought to be naturalized citizens if they live over here?

MR. MARTIN. Yes, sir. I don't know whether it will do any good because we have lots of naturalized citizens now that ought to be deported.

SENATOR McKELLAR. I think that is true, too.

MR. MARTIN. With some the papers do not do them any good. The papers just serve as a protection, that is all. If I had my way I would pick Mr. Foster and his like up, have them examined and if they were convicted of being monomaniacs and a menace to society, I would lock them up, because they are bringing suffering not only upon the Government, but they are bringing suffering upon a lot of poor, innocent, ignorant people, which is unwarranted, and will lead nowhere.

The American Federation of Labor, so far as I have known them, have always worked along constructive lines, always with an aim of going forward. But this strike here seems to me to be just a move to bring things to a standstill and commence destruction. That is my best idea of the matter.

GEORGE MIKULVICH

THE CHAIRMAN. What is your name?

MR. MIKULVICH. George Mikulvich.

THE CHAIRMAN. And what is your nationality?

MR. MIKULVICH. Dalmatian.

THE CHAIRMAN. And were you working down on the coke works before the strike?

MR. MIKULVICH. Yes.

THE CHAIRMAN. How long have you been out on strike?

MR. MIKULVICH. Since the first day it started.

THE CHAIRMAN. September 22?

MR. MIKULVICH. Three weeks.

THE CHAIRMAN. Are you an American citizen?

MR. MIKULVICH. No.

THE CHAIRMAN. How long have you been in this country, Mr. Mikulvich?

MR. MIKULVICH. Seven years.

THE CHAIRMAN. What is the strike for? How did you happen to go on strike?

SENATOR McKELLAR. How much money did you get? How much did you get a day?

MR. MIKULVICH. Forty-two cents an hour.

THE CHAIRMAN. How many hours did you work?

MR. MIKULVICH. Twelve hours and 14 hours.

THE CHAIRMAN. Did you get time and a half overtime?

MR. MIKULVICH. No.

SENATOR McKELLAR. You just get straight 42 cents an hour?

MR. MIKULVICH. Yes.

THE CHAIRMAN. And after you worked 8 hours and worked on 14 hours, did you not get time and a half?

MR. MIKULVICH. No, sir; none of us got time and a half.

THE CHAIRMAN. Well, what are the reasons you struck? We want to know

Ibid., pp. 523–524.

just exactly your side of it. We would
like to hear from you why it was that
you boys struck.

(Mr. Mikulvich did not answer, and
the balance of his statement was taken
through an interpreter). . . .

THE INTERPRETER. He said that he
wanted—that the reason why these people went out on strike and he went with
them was because they wanted to work
shorter hours and get more money and
better conditions in the mill; better
treatment from the bosses and the foremen.

SENATOR McKELLAR. What he wants
is better treatment?

THE INTERPRETER. Yes, sir.

SENATOR McKELLAR. What does he
mean by that?

THE INTERPRETER. The wrong treatment is given to him.

CONCLUSIONS OF THE SENATE COMMITTEE INVESTIGATING THE STRIKE IN THE STEEL INDUSTRIES

ON the 23d day of September, 1919, the Senate passed a resolution instructing the Committee on Education and Labor of the Senate immediately to investigate the steel strike and report to the Senate within the shortest possible time the cause and reason therefor.

The committee, acting through a subcommittee, visited the strike region in western Pennsylvania; went through a number of the mills; talked with the men working in the mills and with the strikers; visited homes of the men and heard evidence for two days at Pittsburgh.

Rather extended hearings have also been held in Washington, and approximately 100 witnesses have been examined. The committee has heard from both sides of the controversy and tried in every way to secure the facts bearing upon this situation. . . .

Wages

The question of wages is not involved in the controversy. Few of the witnesses examined made any complaint as to wages. Some of them did contend that they should have 12-hour pay for 8-hour work, but most of them, while striking for an 8-hour day, claimed only a fair living wage. It is the opinion of the committee that, broadly speaking, the employees of the steel industry at the time of the strike were fairly well satisfied with the wages received, and that such question was not persuasive at all in any consideration of a strike.

The average wages in July, 1919, were $6.27 per day. The wages of unskilled labor in 1914 for a 10-hour day were $2; in 1919, for a 10-hour day, $4.62. In July, 1914, the wages were $2.40; in July, 1919, for a 12-hour day the wages were $5.88. The lowest wage paid to grown men is 42 cents an hour for 8 hours, and 63 cents per hour, or time and a half, for all time over 8 hours. The lowest paid wages for unskilled labor is $4.62 per day.

It may also be said that most of the men speak highly of such homes as are furnished by the company. There is undoubtedly great need of more homes to be sold to the men in order to encourage home owning. They rent these homes at very reasonable prices, and the general condition of these homes seems fairly good.

We find also little complaint as to lack of safety appliances, as to improved machinery, or as to conditions in general outside of the long hours of work. In encouraging and assisting its employees to become owners of its stock; in guarding its employees against accidental injuries; in caring for the sick; and in sanitary precautions generally the work of the United States Steel Corporation at the present time is in the main admirable, and in refreshing contrast to the shortsighted selfishness that still persists in many manufacturing concerns.

From *Hearings before the Committee on Education and Labor, U.S. Senate, Sixty-sixth Congress, Pursuant to S. Res. 188* (Washington, Government Printing Office, 1919), pp. 1, 9–18, 21, 22, 24, 25.

Causes of the Strike

The underlying cause of the strike is the determination of the American Federation of Labor to organize the steel workers in opposition to the known and long-established policy of the steel industry against unionization. . . . The seizing upon this cause by some radicals who are seeking to elevate themselves to power in the American Federation of Labor will be discussed later, but were it not for the attempt to unionize the mills the strike in all probability would not have occurred.

Other reasons are presented by the labor leaders and the laboring men who have gone on the strike, such as—

(a) The refusal of Mr. Gary to confer with the committee claiming to represent the employees. . . . Mr. Fitzpatrick gives this as the reason why the strike was called.

(b) The denial of the right of the employees to be heard by their own representatives through spokesmen of their own choosing. . . .

(c) The demand for the right of collective bargaining to be brought about through unionization of the steel plants.

(d) The demand for an eight-hour day.

(e) The 12 demands of the organizers.

We think, however, that those above mentioned, including subdivisions (a), (b), (c), and (d) are the fundamental ones, and that the other demands, included under (e), were not sufficient, in the judgment even of the employees, to warrant any strike.

The Steel Co.'s Claim as to Reasons for the Strike

(a) Attempt to make plants closed shops by unionizing.

(b) Interference of outsiders who do not represent the men employed and were not themselves workers in the mills.

(c) Radical elements bringing about the strike in order to secure control of the American Federation of Labor, backed by anarchists, Bolshevists, and I.W.W.'s.

It seems to us that this fairly represents the Steel Co.'s position as to the reasons for the strike.

The Steel Co.'s Answer to Labor's Claims

(a) That the men who desired the conference did not represent the employees. Judge Gary . . . claims that these men had not been asked to represent the employees; that they were outside volunteers, and in any event . . . he would not confer with representatives of the unions.

From the testimony:

SENATOR WALSH. You have no objection to unions in your plants. Is that right?

MR. GARY. I do not know what you mean by that.

SENATOR WALSH. You recognize the right of the men to form unions?

MR. GARY. Yes.

SENATOR WALSH. But you refuse to confer with the representatives of the unions?

MR. GARY. Yes. . . .

(b) Answering the eight-hour day claim, the Steel Co. contends it is impossible to have the three shifts; that they can not get the men. An eight-hour day would mean three shifts instead of two. That they have adopted a basic eight-hour day as to pay; that the company is considering the question of establishing an eight-hour day.

(c) That the object of the organizers in unionizing the shops was to bring about a closed shop and that a closed shop means lessening of production.

With Judge Gary (and we speak of him as representing the Steel Co.) this seems to be the most important proposition. On page 170 of the evidence appears this:

SENATOR BORAH. Mr. Gary, this matter all resolves itself then into the single issue, stripped of everything else, that your organization does not propose to deal with representatives of unions as representatives of unions for the reason that you conceive that that would destroy the principle of the open shop?

MR. GARY. Yes; that is true in every respect.

SENATOR BORAH. That is the whole thing in a nutshell.

MR. GARY. Yes; that is a good statement of it. . . .

On the other hand both Mr. Fitzpatrick and Mr. Gompers contend that the open or closed shop is not an issue. On pages 101 and 102 of the hearings Mr. Gompers testified as follows:

MR. GOMPERS. In my letter and the several letters addressed to Judge Gary by the committee there was not the remotest reference to any question of closed shop or open shop. I assert, without any hesitation or fear of contradiction, that it was not in the minds of the committee and I know it was not in the mind of myself, to discuss the question of the open and closed shop if such conference were had. It has been simply—if I may use the vulgarism—lugged in by the judge in that letter that is read and in the publicity of the corporation that this controversy—

THE CHAIRMAN (interrupting). Then you say that the closed shop is not an issue in this strike?

MR. GOMPERS. It is not an issue, sir. You can imagine one of the common laborers, unskilled laborers, or skilled workers, if you please, as an individual, going to Judge Gary and presenting a grievance; or, even if not to Judge Gary, to the corporation's counsel, appointed by Judge Gary. You can imagine what chance of presentation would be afforded such poor devil by the representative of this millions and millions of dollars corporation. You can imagine how much courage a man would have in appearing before Judge Gary, or one of his representatives, to present either an individual grievance or a general grievance which the workers may have.

(d) That a large proportion of the strikers are foreigners; that few Americans have gone out on the strike and that most of the foreigners do not know the reasons for the strike, but have merely followed the agitators and organizers who have held out to them all sorts of alluring promises as to what they would secure by a strike.

Labor's Answer to the Contention of the Steel Co.

(a) That a union shop is not necessarily a closed shop, and that the closed shop was not in any of the demands presented at the conference known as "the 12 demands." . . . That in any event the question of closed shop could not arise until the plants had been unionized, and that Judge Gary's claim that the issue was either the closed or open shop was at least premature because that question could not arise until after the plants were unionized.

(b) That as to outsiders, the men were regular organizers; that while they are from a distance and do not work in the mills, that nevertheless they are selected to speak for the various labor organizations and that labor is entitled to be represented by the best it can secure, whether it be men working with them in the mills or men from without; that the strike shows they do represent a large proportion of the men as indicated by those who have gone out on the strike, which the labor leaders contend is over 200,000.

While they admit that a large percentage of the strikers are foreigners, and that there are some radical elements in their ranks, yet they contend that these radical elements in no way dominate or have had anything to do with bringing about the strike. That if there are a large number of foreigners working in the mills, which is admitted, that the Steel Co. and other large concerns are responsible for bringing them in and can not now be heard to blame them for the troubles brought about.

Such are the various claims of the parties to this dispute. Immediately prior to and during the strike it is also claimed upon the part of the labor representatives that free speech has been suppressed; that the right to meet and discuss their affairs has been denied to the men. Complaint is also made of the conduct during the strike of the State constabulary of Pennsylvania; that their methods have been brutal and unwarranted. Complaint is also made of the conduct of some of the lower magisterial courts in Pennsylvania in the forfeiting of bonds and the refusal to grant the right of counsel, and generally unfair conduct of cases as affecting strikers.

Failure to Postpone Strike

It would seem that the request of the President of the United States, backed up to a large degree by the request of the president of the American Federation of Labor to postpone the strike, should have been complied with. It is hardly sufficient answer to say that Judge Gary likewise declined to accede to the request of the President of the United States that he confer with the claimed representatives of the laborers of the United States Steel Co. with relation to the strike. Both parties, it seems to us, are at fault in refusing to heed the request of the President, and evidences

upon both sides a lack of that consideration for that great third party, the public, which is always the greatest sufferer in a strike of this character. The refusal of the labor leaders who seem to have been the guiding spirits of this strike to accede to the request of the President, even when backed to a certain degree by the president of the American Federation of Labor, lends weight to the idea that radical leadership, instead of conservative leadership, was taking possession of and guiding this particular strike. We regret that Mr. Gompers did not take a firmer position as to postponement.

I

In a hearing of this character, where there are many diverse questions arising, it is natural that there be differences of opinion on the part of the committee as to some of them. Some of the most difficult and far-reaching problems of our industrial life come to the front as issues in this strike. Upon some of them there is a difference of opinion among the various members of the committee. Some of these questions will be discussed later in the report. The committee, however, present these propositions:

(a) That the laborers in the steel mills had a just complaint relative to the long hours of service on the part of some of them and the right to have that complaint heard by the company.

(b) That they had the right to have the representatives of their own choosing present grievances to the employers. Some members of the committee believe that more friendly relations would be maintained between employer and employee if the representatives who are chosen to present grievances to the employers were actually working in the industry and that such representatives ought not to be from outside of the industry.

(c) That behind this strike is massed a considerable element of I.W.W.'s, anarchists, revolutionists, and Russian soviets, and that some radical men not in harmony with the conservative elements of the American Federation of Labor are attempting to use the strike as a means of elevating themselves to power within the ranks of organized labor.

A few suggestions as to these findings will be in order. The evidence disclosed that a percentage of the men work 8 hours, a larger percentage 10 hours, and a lesser percentage 12 hours, although there is dispute in the evidence as to this proposition.

Judge Gary testifies that 34.8 per cent work 8 hours; 39.40 per cent work 10 hours; 26.52 per cent work 12 hours.

We believe that a large majority of the men actually working in the mills work 10 and 12 hours per day. While there are spells of rest here and there through these long periods of 10 and 12 hours, yet the fact remains that the general rule is either a 10- or 12-hour day, during which the men are on duty.

There has been some improvement in the steel industry in this respect, for some years ago a large percentage of the labor worked 10 and 12 hours a day and 7 days in the week. While the claim is made that the 7-day week has been abolished except in emergencies and the men who work on Sundays are allowed one week-day for rest, the evidence on this point is conflicting.

We believe where continuous operation is absolutely necessary the men should at least be allowed one day's rest in each week.

The work in the steel mills is such that men must be constantly in attendance and the work does not stop. To change to an 8-hour day would mean three shifts instead of two. The Steel Co. claims that it is impossible to get the men. And further, that the men want to work more than 8 hours in order to get the additional pay, there being a basic 8-hour day as far as pay is concerned, and time and a half for all time over 8 hours.

It is true some of the workers testified that they wanted to work longer in order to get the increased compensation, but most of them seemed anxious for an 8-hour day with a living wage. The policy of working men 10 and 12 hours per day in the steel mills is, it seems to the committee, an unwise and un-American policy. There are many hundreds of thousands of employees in the steel mills, a considerable portion who can not read, speak, or write the English language. It is claimed by the Steel Co. that a very large proportion of those who are out on the strike are foreigners, which is defined in the evidence to be non-English-speaking people. The testimony sustains this contention.

The 8-hour day is involved in the solution of this question. These non-English-speaking aliens must be Americanized and must learn our language, so the question of a reasonable working day is involved in the question of Americanization. Men can not work 10 and 12 hours per day and attend classes at night school. It is the general consensus of opinion of the best economic writers and thinkers that the establishment of 8-hour-day systems does not diminish production. Nor do we think the claim made that an 8-hour day is impossible because the workmen cannot be secured for three shifts is tenable. An 8-hour day with a living wage that will enable men to support their families and bring up

their children according to the standards
of American life ought to be a cardinal
part of our industrial policy and the
sooner the principle is recognized the
better it will be for the entire country.

The public also has an interest in the
problem of an 8-hour day. Fatigue in
human kind is a breeder of unrest and
dissatisfaction.

II

As to subdivision (b) of the findings
of the committee, namely, the right of
the men to select their own representatives to present their grievances, there
should perhaps be an exception made.
The representatives selected should be
those who believe in the principles of
the American Government. In the instance of Judge Gary refusing to receive
a committee claiming to represent the
men in the employment of the company,
he could well have objected to receiving
a man with the views of Mr. Foster. He
did not put his refusal on that ground,
but put it rather on the ground that the
men did not represent the employees,
though himself conceding that 10 to 15
per cent of the mills were probably
unionized. It seems to us that even 10 to
15 per cent of the men had the right to
select their own representatives and present their grievances to the steel company, and that they should have been
heard. Judge Gary could have announced to them, as well as he did afterwards in his letters to the presidents of
his subsidiary companies, that he would
not deal with representatives of the unions, and that he considered the question
one of open and closed shop; likewise,
it seems to us unfortunate that Mr. Gary
did not answer the letter of Samuel
Gompers, the accredited representative
of the American Federation of Labor
and president thereof. Such things do
not tend to harmonize conditions but rather to accentuate them. The proposition
under discussion raises the question of
collective bargaining, unionism, closed
and open shop, and on these propositions there is much controversy.

The committee is agreed that the
principle of collective bargaining is a
right of men working in industry. Collective bargaining has generally been
recognized as a right of labor. It is apparently one of the effective methods
that labor has used to secure its rights.
The right of collective bargaining, however, should not be employed for the purpose of discriminating against any class
of workmen whether union or nonunion
men. Furthermore, the right when exercised should involve full responsibility
on either side to abide by the terms of
the bargain.

Judge Gary seems to believe that the
question of open and closed shop is involved in the general proposition. There
may be two kinds of closed shop as we
understand it—a shop closed against
nonunion men because they do not belong to a union and a shop closed
against union men because they do belong to a union. One is a closed shop
through the instrumentality of the men
themselves who belong to the union and
the other is a closed shop through the
instrumentality of the employers. Both
of such closed shops are un-American.
The testimony taken does not disclose
either class of closed shop existing in
the steel industry. Men have the right in
this country to work whether they belong to unions or not and no body of
men has the right to stop other men
working because they do not belong to a
union. On the other hand, men have the
right to join unions and to speak through
their unions, and employers have no
right to prevent joining unions or to dis-

charge men or make their positions untenable or unpleasant because they have done so. The doctrine of collective bargaining as generally understood is not recognized in the steel mills, and this has caused considerable dissatisfaction upon the part of many of the steel workers. The question of the open and closed shop would not be involved except indirectly until in fact there was a substantial unionization of the plants. However, Judge Gary takes the position that the organization and unionization of the plants of necessity results in the closed shop. The difficult proposition in this matter continually arising is this: Does collective bargaining through union representatives result in a closed shop? If the unions would recognize the right of men to work and be treated as fellow workers even though they do not belong to the unions, it would not of necessity result in a closed shop. The question is one of great difficulty and the solution of it is not necessary in the view of the committee in order to present a report of conditions.

The committee not being entirely of one mind on the subject presents the facts and the variety of opinions to the Senate.

III

The testimony as introduced and the study the committee has made of the situation lead them to the conclusion that while there were legitimate complaints as to long hours of service, that the strike has been seized upon by some I.W.W.'s, Bolshevists, and anarchists to further their own interests, and that their influence in the strike has been powerful.

The committee is of the opinion that the American Federation of Labor has made a serious mistake and has lost much favorable public opinion which otherwise they would possess by permitting the leadership of this strike movement to pass into the hands of some who heretofore have entertained most radical and dangerous doctrines. If labor is to retain the confidence of that large element of our population which affiliates neither with labor organizations nor capital, it must keep men who entertain and formulate un-American doctrines out of its ranks and join with the employers of labor in eliminating this element from the industrial life of our Nation. Unquestionably, the United States Steel Corporation has had the support of a larger and of a wider circle in the country during the strike because of the character of some of the strike leadership. Labor organizations should not place the workingmen in the position of any sympathy with un-American doctrines or make them followers of any such leadership. Such practice will result in defeating the accomplishment of their demands.

Take the case of Mr. William Z. Foster. Mr. Foster is secretary to the committee composed of the 24 international unions managing this strike. His duties were substantially to act as secretary of the strike, to look after the organization of workers, and to handle the finances. He is in the office at Pittsburgh and seems to be the general manager of the strike. While it is claimed that he has had little to do with it, it is quite apparent to the committee that he has more to do with it than any other man in its actual management. He is one of the signers of the letter to the President and to Mr. Gary. He appears to be a man of excellent education, a thinker, and prolific writer. It is a source of regret to find that a man born in America should have written such doctrines as are set forth in his "Syndicalism" and his more recent publications. At the time of his writing "Syndicalism" he was wholly antagonistic to American labor unions, and especially to the American Federation of Labor. Soon after, however, he seems to have come to the conclusion that he could accomplish his aims and purposes better by boring from within, as he expressed it in one letter to Solidarity, the I.W.W. publication. Carrying out his doctrine of "boring from within" he became active in organized-labor work and soon became a leader.

We insert excerpts from his book showing that he believed that nothing was illegal if necessary to carry out his views. He advocated violence in strikes. He charged the American labor movement was infested with hordes of dishonest officials. He was closely associated with Mr. Margolis, present attorney for the I.W.W.'s at Pittsburgh, who has been behind this strike with all of his power; with Mr. Vincent St. John, formerly secretary to the I.W.W.'s, and the evidence convinces the committee there has been little change of heart on the part of Mr. Foster and that he is now in the full heyday of his power in the "boring from within" process.

Such men are dangerous to the country and they are dangerous to the cause of union labor. It is unfair to men who may be struggling for their rights to be represented by such leaders. It prevents them from securing proper hearing for their cause. If Mr. Foster has the real interest of the laboring man at heart he should remove himself from any leadership. His leadership injures instead of helps. If he will not remove himself from leadership the American Federation of Labor should purge itself of such leadership in order to sustain the confidence which the country has had in it under the leadership of Mr. Gompers.

Labor has done a great work in the war. It has stood nobly by the purposes of this country. It can not now afford to harbor men who in their hearts desire to destroy this Government. . . .

. . . The laborers were contending for American principles in contending for an eight-hour day. They can not put the management of a campaign for American principles into the hands of men who do not believe in American doctrines and hope to succeed.

There may be, in view of the radical utterances and actions of certain leaders, some warrant for the belief that the strike in the steel industry is a part of a general scheme and purpose on the part of radical leaders to bring about a general industrial revolution. The committee, however, do not go to that extent because they feel there were some real grievances. While Mr. Gompers did not originally participate in counseling or advising the strike, he subsequently indorsed it and put the power of his influence behind it. In view of his standing and patriotism the committee does not believe that he could be a participant in a movement involving such revolution. . . .

Since the strike there has been complaint that the strikers have been denied the right of free speech, and that the treatment by the officers has been brutal and that their treatment in the courts does not accord with the high ideals of American democracy. In some places all meetings have been denied. In others street meetings have been denied and indoor meetings permitted. The orders of the mayors and burgesses that no outdoor public meetings, or, in some places, no public meetings should be held, was most distasteful to them. While apparently they were trying to obey this order, they regard it as aimed wholly at them. They are to be commended for their observance of law and order. It may be open to question whether permits to hold meetings should have been denied to the workers, and while generally the orders denying permits were obeyed, yet in most instances where clashes occurred or arrests made it was because of attempts to hold meetings after the request for a permit had been denied.

Freedom of speech is one of the bulwarks of American liberty. Freedom of speech does not, however, mean unbridled license. It does not mean the right of men to advocate the overthrow of this Government, but it seems to us that where a strike is carried on in a peaceful way that the least possible amount of restraint and the largest freedom of speech where meetings are conducted in an orderly way is certainly to be desired in the American Republic. The suppression of frank discussion only serves to accentuate a bad situation.

Officials should not hesitate to prevent meetings called together for the purpose of advocating the overthrow of the Government. On the other hand, they ought not to be permitted to prevent men meeting and talking over their grievances and presenting to the men their arguments in favor of joining the union or refraining from joining the union. Incidents have been presented to the committee of unnecessary force by police officers. Probably there will always be abuses in times of excitement, but apparently there have been cases of unoffending men and women arrested without reason by the officers, put into jail, and in some cases fined by magistrates without warrant or justification. It is not necessary to refer to special cases as disclosed by the evidence. The action in many instances was such as to lead one side of this controversy to the belief that the officers of the law were acting on the side of the Steel Co. Such a situation is unfortunate and helps to breed discontent. As long as officers are human beings they will make mistakes. They should be very careful that in maintaining the majesty and dignity of the law they do nothing to bring it into disrespect.

As to the complaint of the action of the courts, we are inclined to believe that there is some ground for complaint and that the magisterial courts in the taking of bonds and the forfeiting of bonds, in the arresting of people merely as suspicious characters and sending them to jail therefor, has not in every instance been justifiable. The courts should be very careful that they are not subject to just criticism for curtailing the rights of defendants.

The foreigners whom the needs of our industries bring among us can not be dragooned into love for America and loyalty to its institutions. Public officials should always be ready to receive sympathetic suggestions for the relief of just complaints or violations of or interference with the legal or humane rights of labor, as well as the insistence upon a protection of the property rights of capital and the preservation of law and order.

. . . There is a third party, however, to all of this controversy—the great public. There is no place in this country either for industrial despotism or labor despotism. No one should be permitted to unjustly cause the great body of the public to suffer. Strikes are a relic of industrial barbarism, but at present strikes are apparently the only way for labor to secure even its just demands if employers refuse to grant them or to submit them to arbitration. It is not to the credit of our Nation that no way has been devised to settle these disputes outside of strikes. They are destructive and wrecking to the industrial life of the Nation. Somebody has to pay the bill and in every instance it is the public. The public has a right to demand that capital shall not arrogate to itself the right to determine in its own way these industrial questions, and it is the same as to labor, and the duty is upon the Congress as representing the people to provide some means for the adjustment of these difficulties. . . .

William Z. Foster: ANALYSIS OF THE SENATE COMMITTEE REPORT

UPON November 8, the Senate Committee, having completed its hearings, made public its report. This document is a strange mixture of progressive and reactionary principles. In some respects, especially where it grants, however confusedly, the right of collective bargaining and the eight hour day, it is just and meets the situation; but in other respects it is so unfair to the workers' cause as to be grotesque. For one thing it shoulders upon the unions the entire responsibility for the failure to postpone the strike, choosing to disregard completely the clearly established fact that the steel companies were discharging men so fast that for the unions it was a case of strike or perish. In fact, the report ignores altogether the bitter grievance of men being discharged for union membership. Mr. Gary had said that this practice was not engaged in, and that apparently settled it so far as the Committee was concerned,—the testimony of dozens of victimized workers (with thousands more available) to the contrary notwithstanding. Other sins of the Steel Trust, the suppression of free speech and free assembly, etc., were passed over lightly; but the alleged virtues of its housing and welfare plans were very highly lauded.

Nowhere are the workers more ruthlessly robbed and exploited by their employers than in the steel industry. Speaking recently in Brooklyn on the subject of profiteering, Mr. Basil Manly, formerly Joint Chairman of the National War Labor Board, cited Page 367 of the Treasury report as showing one steel company "earning" $14,549,952 in 1917 on a capital of $5,000, or a profit of 290,999 per cent. As the department conveniently suppresses all details, it is impossible to learn the name of this company or how it made such fabulous profits. On the same page appeared another steel company with a profit rate of 20,180 per cent. Speaking of the United States Steel Corporation's returns, which of course were garbled so that no outsider could understand them, Mr. Manly said:

For this reason I am unable to tell you, on the basis of the Treasury Department's figures, what the net income of the Steel Corporation is, but on the basis of its own published report I can tell you that in two years, 1916 and 1917, the net profits of the Steel Corporation, after payment of interest on bonds and after making allowance for all charges growing out of the installation of special war facilities, amounted to $888,931,511. This is more by $20,000,000 than the total capital stock of the Steel Corporation (which is $868,583,600). In other words, in 1916 and 1917 every dollar of the capital stock of the Steel Corporation was paid for in net profits. In this connection it should be remembered that when the Steel Corporation was formed its entire $500,000,000 worth of common stock represented nothing but water.

The other steel companies did as well or better, proportionately. W. Jett Lauck, acting on behalf of the railroad workers, submitted figures to the United States

From *The Great Steel Strike and Its Lessons* by William Z. Foster, pp. 149–154, 241–243, 256–260. Copyright 1920 by B. W. Heubsch, Inc. Reprinted by permission of The Viking Press, Inc.

Railroad Labor Board (A.P. dispatches May 19, 1920) showing that during the years 1916–18 the Bethlehem Steel Corporation "earned" average annual profits of $29,000,000, or six times its pre-war average. In 1916 its profits amounted to 146 per cent on its capital stock. Our Johnstown friend, the Cambria Steel Company, in 1916–17 cleaned up $50,000,000 on $45,000,000 capital stock; while Lackawanna, Republic, Colorado Fuel and Iron, Jones and Laughlin, Crucible, etc., companies, made similar killings.

As against useless, non-producing drones getting these millions, the great mass of workers actually operating the industry were receiving the beggarly wages of from 42 to 48 cents per hour. They had received no increase for a year before the strike, notwithstanding the skyrocketing cost of living. Yet the Senate Committee could discover no discontent at this condition nor see any injustice in it. Upon page 10 of its report appears the startling statement that "The question of wages is not involved in this controversy." Forty-two cents an hour would hardly buy cigars for these smug, well-fed gentlemen; still they would have us conclude that it is enough for a steel worker to raise a family upon.

The fact is, of course, that an increase in wages was a cardinal demand of the strikers, even though the Senate Committee did not get to learn of it. And so great was the steel workers' need for more money that the strike had scarcely ended when the United States Steel Corporation, followed soon after by the "independents," granted its lesser skilled help 10 per cent increase in wages, and promised "an equitable adjustment" to the widely advertised small minority of highly paid men.

Part of the strike-bearing strategy of the Steel Trust was to alienate public sympathy from the strike by denouncing it as an incipient revolution which had to be put down at all costs. Public opinion was already violently inflamed against everything savoring no matter how slightly of radicalism, and it was not difficult for the re-actionary newspapers to make the steel strike unpopular, even as they had, under various pretexts, the movements of the miners and railroad men of the period. One weapon they used extensively against the steel strike was an almost forgotten pamphlet, "Syndicalism," written by Earl C. Ford and myself eight years ago.

Throughout the hearings the investigating senators went along with this Steel Trust propaganda, which was not so surprising considering the fact that of the five active committee men, one was a steel magnate, and three others typical Bourbons. By playing up the "little red book" they systematically fed the newspapers with the sensationalism they wanted and which the steel companies desired them to get. I was called before the Committee and gruffly ordered to express my opinion on the doctrines in the booklet. In reply, I stated that the steel movement had been carried on according to the strictest trade-union principles. It was overseen by the National Committee, consisting of twenty-four presidents of large international unions. As secretary of this committee I had necessarily worked under the close scrutiny of these men and dozens of their organizers—not to speak of the highest officials in the American Federation of Labor. Yet none of these trade unionists, keen though they be to detect and condemn unusual practices and heresy in the ranks, had found fault with the character of my work. Nor could the crew of detectives and stool pigeons of the steel companies and Department of Justice, who had dogged my footsteps for a year past, cite a single word said, a thing done, or a line written by me in the entire campaign which would not measure up to most rigid trade-union standards. I contended that my private opinions were immaterial as they did not and could not enter into the organizing work or the strike.

But the nation-wide head hunt of the radicals was on in full cry, and the Senators had a good blood scent. They would follow it to the end. They insisted that I express my opinion upon the wage system, the state, morality, patriotism, marriage, etc. Finally, in a last effort to protect the interests of the 2,000,000 men, women and children affected by the strike, I stated that if the vulture press, which was bound to misrepresent what I said, was removed from the room, I would be glad to oblige the Senators with a frank expression of my views upon any subject. But this simple fairness to the steel workers and their families they denied. The newspapers were clamoring for red meat, and the Senators seemed determined they should have it. Having made my protest and my prediction, I was compelled to yield; but the first newspapers on the streets proved the soundness of my fears. My answers were garbled and twisted against both the steel movement and me. . . .

Radical Leadership as a Strike Issue

In order to cover up their own inveterate opposition to Organized Labor in all its forms and activities, and to blind the workers to the real cause of the defeat, namely lack of sufficient power on the employees' side, great employing interests caused to be spread over the whole country the statement that the steel strike failed because of radical leadership, and that if such "dangerous" men as John Fitzpatrick and myself had not been connected with it everything would have been lovely. They were especially severe against me for my "evil" influence on the strike. But somehow their propaganda did not seem to strike root among labor men, especially those who were backing the steel campaign. . . .

As for myself, and I know John Fitzpatrick took the same position regarding himself, I was willing to resign my position on the National Committee the very instant it was indicated by those associated with me that my presence was injuring the movement. I felt that to be my duty. But to the last, that indication never came. . . .

Moreover, at any time in the campaign a word from the executive officers of the A.F. of L. would have brought about my resignation. This they were aware of for months before the strike. All of which indicates that the men responsible for the organizations in the movement were satisfied that it was being carried on according to trade-union principles, and also that in consideration of the Steel Trust's murderous tactics in the past it was a certainty that if the opposition had not taken the specific form it did, it would have manifested itself in some other way as bad or worse. It was to be depended upon that some means would have been found to thoroughly discredit the movement.

This conviction was intensified by the unexampled fury with which each important move of Labor during the past year has been opposed, not only by employers but by governmental officials as well. All through the war the moneyed interests watched with undisguised alarm and hatred the rapid advance of the unions; but they were powerless to stop it. Now, however, they are getting their revenge. The usual method of defeating such movements during this period of white terrorism is to attach some stigma to them; to question the legitimacy of their aims, and then, when the highly organized and corrupted press has turned public sentiment against them, to crush them by the most unscrupulous means. It makes no difference how mild or ordinary the movement is, some issue is always found to poison public opinion against it. . . .

Are the Trade Unions Revolutionary?

For many years radicals in this country have almost universally maintained that the trade unions are fundamentally non-revolutionary; that they have no real quarrel with capitalism, but are seeking merely to modify its harshness through a policy of mild reform. They have been pictured as lacking both the intelligence to want industrial freedom and the courage to demand it. And so often have these ideas been repeated, so slight has been the inquiry into their soundness, that they have come to be accepted in a large degree by virtually the entire left wing of the labor movement. To these ideas, more than anything else, is due the current idealistic labor pessimism, the unsympathetic attitude toward, and general lack of understanding of, the trade unions.

Yet their falsity is readily apparent when one takes into consideration the real situation. It is an undisputable fact that the trade unions always act upon the policy of taking all they can get from their exploiters. They even overreach themselves sometimes, as a thousand lost strikes eloquently testify. Their program is directly anti-capitalistic. But let me quote from a booklet, written by myself several years ago, entitled, "Trade Unionism; the Road to Freedom," page 18:

It is idle to say that the trade unions will rest content with anything short of actual emancipation. For they are as insatiable as the veriest so-called revolutionary unions. In the measure that their strength increases, so do their demands. They have sent wages up: 2, 3, 4, 5, 6, 7, 8 dollars per day, and hours down: 12, 11, 10, 9, 8, 7, 6, per day with all kinds of other concessions sandwiched in between. And now they are more radical in their demands than ever before in their history. Permanently satisfied trade unions under capitalism would be the eighth wonder of the world, outrivalling in interest the famous hanging gardens of Babylon. They would be impossible. With its growing power, Organized Labor will go on winning greater and greater concessions, regardless of how profound they may be. It is purest assumption to state that the trade unions would balk at ending the wages system.

So far as the tendency of their demands is concerned, there can be no question about that to anyone who will look at them squarely; the trade unions may be depended upon always to check exploitation through the wages system as far as their power enables them. The big question is whether or not they will be able to develop enough power to stop this exploitation altogether. As for me, I am confident that they will. In every country they are constantly adding to and solidifying their ranks; building ever more gigantic and militant combinations and throwing them athwart the exploiter's path. It is safe to say that if they cannot finally stop him it will be because it does not lie within the realms of possibility for the working class to produce a sufficiently powerful organization.

Why, then, have these strongly anti-capitalistic qualities been so long and generally ignored and the trade unions considered merely as palliative bodies? In my opinion it is because they, like various other aggressive social movements, have more or less instinctively surrounded themselves with a sort of camouflage or protective coloring, designed to disguise the movement and thus to pacify and disarm the opposition. This is the function of such expressions as, "A fair day's pay for a fair day's work," "The interests of Capital and Labor are identical," etc. In actual practice little or no attention is paid to them. They are for foreign consumption. The fact that those who utter them may actually believe what they say does not change the situation a particle. Most movements are blind to their own goals anyway. The important thing is the real trend of the movement, which is indisputably as I have stated above, on the one hand constantly expanding organization, and on the other constantly increasing demands. The trade unions will not *become* anti-capitalistic through the conversion of their members to a certain point of view or by the adoption of certain preambles; they *are* that by their very makeup and methods. The most that can be done is to clarify their aims and intensify their efforts towards freedom.

If the trade unions instinctively throw dust in the eyes of their enemies, they do it for an altogether worthy purpose, the elevation of the standard of well-being for the mass of the people. In the case of the capitalist class we see the same principle applied to an utterly vicious end. The whole trend of the great employing interests is to set up an oligarchy of wealthy parasites, neither toiling nor spinning, yet for whom the whole body of workers would be compelled to labor in degradation and poverty. And if unopposed, they would not only bring about this condition, but in so doing would rob the people of every right they have—free speech, free press, free assemblage, legislative representation, trial by jury, and all the rest. But do they openly avow their purpose? Most asuredly not, for they know that powerful though they are they would be swept away by a wave of popular opposition. Therefore, through their newspapers and innumerable other propaganda agencies, they proceed to cover up their nefarious schemes of exploitation and oppression with hypocritical cloaks of patriotism, religion, benevolence, and the like. Their practice is one thing, their preaching something entirely different. Thus we have Garys and Rockefellers actually enslaving their workers by the most brutal methods and at the same time seeking to convince the public that what they are trying to do is to protect these workers from union domination, to preserve to them their sacred right to work for whomever they please, etc. Men such as these are knifing America and doing it in the name of 100 per cent Americanism. They are social camouflagers par excellence.

CONCLUSIONS AND RECOMMENDATIONS OF INTERCHURCH WORLD MOVEMENT REPORT

THE steel strike of September 22, 1919, to January 7, 1920, in one sense, is not over. The main issues were not settled. The causes still remain. Moreover, both causes and issues remain uncomprehended by the nation. The strike, although the largest in point of numbers in the history of the country up to the first date, exhibited this extraordinary phase: the basic facts concerning the work and lives of the 300,000 strikers were never comprehensively discovered to the public. . . .

Put tersely, the public mind completely lost sight of the real causes of the strike, which lay in hours, wages and conditions of labor, fixed "arbitrarily," according to the head of the United States Steel Corporation, in his testimony at a Senatorial investigation. It lost sight of them because it was more immediately concerned with the actual outcome of the great struggle between aggregations of employers and aggregations of workers than it was with the fundamental circumstances that made such a struggle inevitable. This investigation and report deal primarily with the causative facts,—with abiding conditions in the steel industry—and only secondarily with conflicts of policies and their influence on national institutions and modes of thought.

Out of the first set of undisputed facts, these may be cited in the beginning:

(a) The number of those working the twelve-hour day is 69,000. (Testimony of E. H. Gary, Senate Investigation, Vol. I, p. 157.)

(b) The number of those receiving the common labor or lowest rate of pay is 70,000. (Letters of E. H. Gary to this Commission.)

This means that approximately 350,000[1] men, women and children are directly affected by the longest hours or the smallest pay in that part of the industry owned by the United States Steel Corporation, which fixes pay and hours without conference with the labor force.

Since this corporation controls about half the industry, it is therefore a reasonably conservative estimate that working conditions of three quarters of a million of the nation's population have their lives determined arbitrarily by the twelve-hour day or by the lowest pay in the steel industry.

This nub of the situation, the Commission found, was subordinated, and after the strike remained subordinate, to the industry's warfare over collective bargaining. Both sides were enmeshed. The huge steel companies, committed to a non-union system (and offering no alternative) and the masses of workers, moving as workers do traditionally, seemed both to be helpless. Espionage replaced collective bargaining or cooperative service.

[1] The average American family, the so-called statistical family, consists of five persons.

From The Interchurch World Movement, *Report on the Steel Strike of 1919*, pp. 3–18, 31–36, 38, 39, 41, 44–48, 50–52, 57–60, 65, 144–45, 147–153, 219, 226–27, 233, 236, 238–40. Copyright, 1920, by Harcourt, Brace & World, Inc.

Inauguration of Inquiry

The data for this report were obtained by and for an independent Commission of Inquiry appointed at the request of the Industrial Relations Department of the Interchurch World Movement of North America after a National Industrial Conference in New York on October 3, 1919. The Conference rejected a resolution condemning one party to the strike for refusing to adopt the principle of collective bargaining but unanimously supported a resolution directing a thorough investigation of the strike and publication of the reports of the investigators.

Those parts of the evidence obtained directly by the Commission were secured through personal observation and through open hearings held in Pittsburgh in November, supplemented by inspection trips in Western Pennsylvania, Ohio, Indiana and Illinois. More technical and detailed data were obtained by a staff of investigators working under a field director from the Bureau of Industrial Research, New York. Other evidence was obtained directly by the Bureau of Industrial Research, by the Bureau of Applied Economics in Washington, by a firm of consulting engineers, and by various other organizations and technical experts working under the direction of the Commission. . . .

Difficulties in obtaining evidence were expected;—they exceeded expectations. In certain quarters the Commission of clergymen were charged with being "Bolshevists" and "anarchists"; their investigators were rebuffed as "Reds"; one was "arrested." Formal action was finally necessary to combat the circulation in written form of charges whose only basis, apparently, was that any persons had ventured to make any investigation. In other quarters great courtesy was accorded, coupled with inability to furnish the desired statistics. Moreover the lack of up-to-date and available statistics which should have been possessed by union officials, the over-supply of unverified complaints from strikers and the reluctance to impart any information on the part of the companies combined to lengthen unduly the period of field investigation. . . .

At one period, investigation was delayed by an effort of the Commission to settle the strike. The Commission, having been urged to do so in a manner impossible to refuse, actually formulated a plan of mediation which was formally accepted by the leaders of the strike but was definitely rejected by the Steel Corporation.

Scope and Method

The scope of the inquiry was delimited by applying two simple questions:

(a) What workers constituted the bulk of the strikers?

The answer is not disputed: the backbone of the strike consisted of the mass of common labor and the semi-skilled, constituting roughly three-quarters of all employees, and mostly "foreigners."

By "foreigners" the steel industry means not all immigrants or sons of immigrants, but only the "new immigration," consisting of the score of races from southeastern or eastern Europe. About half of these "foreigners" had citizenship papers.

In many places all the skilled struck; in a few places the skilled went out and many unskilled stayed in the mills.

The foreigners had never been organized before; hitherto they had been looked upon by the unions as potential strike breakers, "stealing Americans' jobs and lowering the American standard of living."

(b) What was the chief factor on the employers' side?

The answer is not in dispute: The U.S. Steel Corporation was the admittedly decisive influence.

Whatever the Steel Corporation does, the rest of the industry will ultimately do; whatever modifications of policy fail to take place in the industry fail because of the opposition of the Steel Corporation.

Throughout the report great emphasis is laid on Mr. Gary's testimony, partly because he was almost the sole spokesman for the industry during the strike and partly because officials, corporation and "independent," referred investigators to Mr. Gary and often limited their own testimony to reading extracts from Mr. Gary's statements or approving his policies.

The *scope* of the inquiry, therefore, included chiefly representative cross-sections of the mass of low-skilled "foreigners" in the Pittsburgh and Chicago district plants of the Steel Corporation.

Of the Corporation's 268,000 employees, 80,000 are miners, railworkers and dockmen, ship crews and shipyard workers, who were untouched by the strike and are therefore excluded.

The *method* was to carry the inquiry to the steel workers themselves, strikers and non-strikers. Effort was made to get beyond the debates of Mr. Gary and Mr. Gompers. The statements and affidavits of 500 steel workers, carefully compared and tested, constitute the rock bottom of the findings, the testimony of the leaders on both sides being used chiefly to interpret these findings.

Effort was made to keep in mind that

a strike is not merely a *call* to strike, it is a *walk-out,* frequently without a call. Everything,—Mr. Gary, Mr. Gompers, the Corporation's labor policies, Mr. Foster's record,—was viewed in the light of whether or not it had or had not a relation to the separation of 300,000 men from their jobs.

The Commission and its investigators went to the steel workers with two main questions:

A. Why did you strike? (Or why refuse to strike?)

B. What do you want?

Answers to A. were found to deal with things that existed,—schedules of hours, wages, conditions, grievances, physical states and states of mind.

Answers to B. were found to deal with a method (hitherto non-existent in the steel industry), for changing A.; the strike leaders called it collective bargaining and the right to organization; the steel employers called it the closed shop and labor autocracy.

Therefore, the first half of the inquiry concerned, primarily, conditions of labor.

The second half concerned, primarily, methods for changing the conditions revealed by the first half.

The second line of inquiry was found to stretch back with decisive effect over the first half; in short, the key to the steel industry, both before and during the strike and now was found in following to its furthest implications this question: What means of conference exist in the steel mills? Both sides agreed that the *occasion* of the strike, leaving aside for the moment its relation to any fundamental cause, was the denial of a conference, requested by organized labor and refused by Mr. Gary.

The inquiry into the means of conference was pursued through the three possible forms of conference: (a) through individuals; (b) through shop committee or company unions; (c) through labor unions.

The complete scope of this phase of the inquiry might be restated as follows:

(A) Investigation of a system of denial of organization and collective bargaining (the policy of the Steel Corporation).

(B) Investigation of a system or systems of non-union collective bargaining (existent in certain "independent" plants where strikes had once existed or were feared).

(C) Investigation of a movement for collective bargaining and organization of the traditional trade union kind (initiated by the American Federation of Labor and fought by the Steel Corporation).

Inquiry B. was not sufficiently completed to be presented in this report, except as a sidelight on the main conditions. The plans in operation or attempted in the Pueblo plant of the Colorado Fuel and Iron Company, the Midvale-Cambria Company, the Bethlehem, Inland and International Harvester plants, etc., did not suggest to the dominant factor, the Steel Corporation, any modification of its policy.

Summarized Conclusions

Sufficient data were analyzed to warrant the following main conclusions concisely stated here and discussed at length in this report and the sub-reports.

1. The conduct of the iron and steel industry was determined by the conditions of labor accepted by the 191,000 employees in the U.S. Steel Corporation's manufacturing plants.
2. These conditions of labor were fixed by the Corporation, without collective bargaining or any functioning means of conference; also without above-board means of learning how the decreed conditions affected the workers.
3. Ultimate control of the plants was vested in a small group of financiers whose relation to the producing force was remote. The financial group's machinery of control gave it full knowledge of output and dividends, but negligible information of working and living conditions.
4. The jobs in the five chief departments of the plants were organized in a pyramid divided roughly into thirds; the top third of skilled men, chiefly Americans, resting on a larger third of semi-skilled, all based on a fluctuating mass of common labor. Promotion was at pleasure of company representatives.
5. Rates of pay and other principal conditions were based on what was accepted by common labor; the unskilled and semi-unskilled force was largely immigrant labor.
6. The causes of the strike lay in the hours, wages and control of jobs and in the manner in which all these were fixed.
7. HOURS. Approximately one-half the employees were subjected to the twelve-hour day. Approximately one-half of these in turn were subjected to the seven-day week.
   Much less than one-quarter had a working day of less than ten hours (sixty-hour week).
   The average week for all employees was 68.7 hours; these employees generally believed that a week of over sixty hours ceased to be a standard in other industries fifteen to twenty years ago.
   Schedules of hours for the chief

classes of steel workers were from twelve to forty hours longer per week than in other basic industries near steel communities; the American steel average was over twenty hours longer than the British, which ran between forty-seven to forty-eight hours in 1919.

Steel jobs were largely classed as heavy labor and hazardous.

The steel companies professed to have restored practically pre-war conditions; the hours nevertheless were longer than in 1914 or 1910. Since 1910 the Steel Corporation has increased the percentage of its twelve-hour workers.

The only reasons for the twelve-hour day, furnished by the companies, were found to be without adequate basis in fact. The increased hours were found to be a natural development of large scale production, which was not restricted by public sentiment or by organization among employees. The twelve-hour day made any attempt at "Americanization" or other civic or individual development for one-half of all immigrant steel workers arithmetically impossible.

8. WAGES. The annual earnings of over one-third of all productive iron and steel workers were, and had been for years, below the level set by government experts as the *minimum of subsistence* standard for families of five. The annual earnings of 72 per cent of all workers were, and had been for years, below the level set by government experts as the *minimum of comfort* level for families of five.

This second standard being the lowest which scientists are willing to term an "American standard of liv-

ing," it follows that nearly three-quarters of the steel workers could not earn enough for an American standard of living. The bulk of unskilled steel labor earned less than enough for the average family's minimum subsistence; the bulk of semi-skilled labor earned less than enough for the average family's minimum comfort.

Skilled steel labor was paid wages disproportionate to the earnings of the other two-thirds, thus binding the skilled class to the companies and creating divisions between the upper third and the rest of the force. Wage rates in the iron and steel industry as a whole are determined by the rates of the U.S. Steel Corporation. The Steel Corporation sets its wage rates, the same as its hour schedules, without conference (or collective bargaining), with its employees.

Concerning the financial ability of the Corporation to pay higher wages the following must be noted (with the understanding that the Commission's investigation did not include analysis of the Corporation's financial organization): the Corporation vastly increased its undistributed financial reserves during the Great War. In 1914 the Corporation's total undivided surplus was $135,204,471.90. In 1919 this total undivided surplus had been increased to $493,048,201.93. Compared with the wage budgets, in 1919, the Corporation's final surplus after paying dividends of $96,382,027 and setting aside $274,277,835 for Federal taxes payable in 1919, was $466,888,421,—a sum large enough to have paid a second time the total wage and salary budget for 1918 ($452,663,524), and to have left a surplus of over $14,000,000. In 1919 the undivided surplus was $493,048,201.93, or $13,000,000 more than the total wage and salary expenditures.

Increases in wages during the war in no case were at a sacrifice of stockholders' dividends.

Extreme congestion and unsanitary living conditions, prevalent in most Pennsylvania steel communities, were largely due to underpayment of semi-skilled and common labor.

9. GRIEVANCES. The Steel Corporation's arbitrary control of hours and wages extended to everything in individual steel jobs, resulting in daily grievances.

The Corporation, committed to a non-union system, was as helpless as the workers to anticipate these grievances.

The grievances, since there existed no working machinery of redress, weighed heavily in the industry, because they incessantly reminded the worker that he had no "say" whatever in steel.

Discrimination against immigrant workers, based on rivalry of economic interests, was furthered by the present system of control and resulted in race divisions within the community.

10. CONTROL. The arbitrary control of the Steel Corporation extended outside the plants, affecting the workers as citizens and the social institutions in the communities.

The steel industry was under the domination of a policy whose aim was to keep out labor unions. In pursuit of this policy, blacklists were used, workmen were discharged for union affiliation, "under-cover men" and "labor detectives" were em-

ployed and efforts were made to influence the local press, pulpit and police authorities.

In Western Pennsylvania the civil rights of free speech and assembly were abrogated without just cause, both for individuals and labor organizations. Personal rights of strikers were violated by the State Constabulary and sheriff's deputies.

Federal authorities, in some cases, acted against groups of workmen on the instigation of employees of steel companies. In many places in Western Pennsylvania, community authorities and institutions were subservient to the maintenance of one corporation's anti-union policies.

11. The organizing campaign of the workers and the strike were for the purpose of forcing a conference in an industry where no means of conference existed; this specific conference to set up trade union collective bargaining, particularly to abolish the twelve-hour day and arbitrary methods of handling employees.

12. No interpretation of the movement as a plot or conspiracy fits the facts; that is, it was a mass movement, in which leadership became of secondary importance.

13. Charges of Bolshevism or of industrial radicalism in the conduct of the strike were without foundation.

14. The chief cause of the defeat of the strike was the size of the Steel Corporation, together with the strength of its active opposition and the support accorded it by employers generally, by governmental agencies and by organs of public opinion.

15. Causes of defeat, second in importance only to the fight waged by the Steel Corporation, lay in the organization and leadership, not so much

of the strike itself, as of the American labor movement.

16. The immigrant steel worker was led to expect more from the twenty-four International Unions of the A.F. of L. conducting the strike than they, through indifference, selfishness or narrow habit, were willing to give.

17. Racial differences among steel workers and an immigrant tendency toward industrial unionism, which was combated by the strike leadership, contributed to the disunity of the strikers.

18. The end of the strike was marked by slowly increasing disruption of the new unions; by bitterness between the "American" and "foreign" worker and by bitterness against the employer, such as to diminish production.

The following question was definitely placed before the Commission of Inquiry: Were the strikers justified? The investigation's data seem to make impossible any other than this conclusion:

The causes of the strike lay in grievances which gave the workers just cause for complaint and for action. These unredressed grievances still exist in the steel industry.

Recommendations

1. Inasmuch as—

(a) conditions in the iron and steel industry depend on the conditions holding good among the workers of the U.S. Steel Corporation, and—

(b) past experience has proved that the industrial policies of large-scale producing concerns are basically influenced by (1) public opinion expressed in governmental action, (2) labor unions,

which in this case have failed, or (3) by both, and—

(c) permanent solutions for the industry can only be reached by the Steel Corporation in free cooperation with its employees, therefore—

It is recommended—

(a) that the Federal Government be requested to initiate the immediate undertaking of such settlement by bringing together both sides;

(b) that the Federal Government, by presidential order or by congressional resolution, set up a commission representing both sides and the public, similar to the Commission resulting from the coal strike; such Commission to—

1. inaugurate immediate conferences between the Steel Corporation and its employees for the elimination of the 12-hour day and the 7-day week, and for the readjustment of wage rates;

2. devise with both sides and establish an adequate plan of permanent free conference to regulate the conduct of the industry in the future;

3. continue and make nationwide and exhaustive this inquiry into basic conditions in the industry.

II. Inasmuch as—

(a) the administration of civil law and police power in Western Pennsylvania has created many injustices which persist, and—

(b) no local influence has succeeded in redressing this condition, therefore—

It is recommended—

(a) that the Federal Government inaugurate full inquiry into the past and present state of civil liberties in Western Pennsylvania and publish the same.

III. Inasmuch as—

(a) the conduct and activities of "labor-detective" agencies do not seem to serve the best interests of the country, and—

(b) the Federal Department of Justice seems to have placed undue reliance on cooperation with corporations' secret services, therefore—

It is recommended—

(a) that the Federal Government institute investigation for the purpose of regulating labor-detective agencies; and for the purpose of publishing what government departments or public moneys are utilized to cooperate with company "under-cover men."

IV. It is recommended that the proper Federal authorities be requested to make public two reports of recent investigations of conditions in the steel industry, in making which public money was spent, and to explain why these and similar reports have not hitherto been made public, and why reports which were printed have been limited to extremely small editions.

The second preliminary phase of the report concerns the charge, widely current, that the strike was a product of Bolshevism. . . .

A stranger in America reading the newspaper during the strike and talking with steel masters both in and out of steel communities must have concluded that the strike represented a serious outbreak of Bolshevism red hot from Russia. . . .

Data on the strike as a Bolshevist manifestation were analyzed with the following questions in mind:

1. Who started this explanation?
2. Why was it offered?
3. Was there Bolshevism in the strike? Was there radicalism?

The allegation was not offered by the strikers nor by the government. It was traced chiefly to two sources: first, the newspapers; and these led to the second and main source, the steel companies.

First, the commission addressed to Mr. Gary, after long discussions with him personally and after considering particularly his statements that men still out were "Bolsheviki," a letter which formally asked him to furnish the evidence on which he based that judgment. The Commission at the time felt confident that Mr. Gary could furnish considerable evidence and that any discussion would turn on whether or not the evidence he produced proved the case. But Mr. Gary produced nothing. . . .

Of the many interviewed, no steel company official presented to the Commission any evidence of Bolshevism. In declaring on December 5 that the workmen who "followed the leadership of Fitzpatrick and Foster were Bolsheviki," Mr. Gary insisted to the Commission that the strike aims were "the closed shop, soviets and the forcible distribution of property." . . .

Mr. Buffington, in supporting Mr. Gary's position, said: "The organizers were all subversive. They said things to make the labor forces want more than fair wages; made 'em want to share the profits."

Mr. Gary was finally asked in the course of one of these discussions if he did not really mean that "labor was getting too strong." To this he gave general assent.

. . . the Commission carefully examined the organization of the strike, and the union literature, listened to speakers, consulted Federal and State officials, and in every way sought to get at the bottom of the Bolshevist theory. The line of inquiry included such questions as: What induced the newspapers in many states in the first week after September 22 to print on their front pages extensive extracts of a pamphlet called "Syndicalism" by Wm. Z. Foster? Why was "radicalism" charged? . . .

The "Red Book's" actual relation to the strike is undisputed. No copy of the original book, out of print for several years, was found in the possession of any striker or strike leader. A reprint, which was a facsimile in everything except the price mark and the union label, was widely circulated from the middle of September on by officials of the steel companies. The absence of the union label indicated that the reprint was not in behalf of any labor organization. What organization bore this expense of reproducing the book was not investigated. There was no need to investigate who distributed it. Steel company officials openly supplied it to newspapers, to preachers and investigators. In McKeesport, for example, it was mailed to all the pastors in the city who were then summoned to a meeting with the Mayor, attended also by representatives of the Sheriff, the State Constabulary and the Steel Corporation. . . .

Attempts to raise the question, "Was Mr. Foster really sincere in recanting Syndicalism?" inevitably raised the other question, "Was Mr. Gary really sincere in charging Bolshevism?" It seemed best to leave such analysis to speculative psychologists.

. . . Only the conclusions need be set down here and these are—

That the control of the movement to organize the steel industry, vested in twenty-four A.F. of L. trade unions, was such that Mr. Foster's acts were perforce in harmony with old line unionism.

That Mr. Foster "harmoniously" combated the natural tendency of sections of the rank and file toward industrial unionism.

That a mass movement involving 300,000 workers and twenty-four national unions cannot be controlled to secret, opposite ends.

The organizing plan was the same and was directed by the same two men as that of the stock yards employees in 1918. That campaign was carried through to recognition of the unions without anyone calling it Bolshevism. The plan rejected the opportunity to organize along the line commonly called the One Big Union. . . .

As to literature: the official strike pronouncements and leaflets were confined to orthodox tests. Investigators saw one bunch of Communist leaflets but these had been confiscated by strike leaders who had thrown the distributor out of a hall into which he had wormed his way. Mr. Foster refused to allow in an official strike bulletin even the mild advice that laboring men should join a labor party, until the chairman of the National Committee, John Fitzpatrick himself, ordered it put in. . . .

No leaders of the strike were convicted of "radicalism" in court. Hundreds of strikers were rounded up in "radical raids," but none tried and convicted. . . .

Were there any radicals in the sense of rebels against their present way of life? The steel industry was full of them. They wanted big changes. But the changes were all related definitely to the right to organize, the twelve-hour day, the seven-day week, the foremen's ways, the company's methods, or some other definite thing which they were sick of. It is possible that the workers throughout the whole steel industry might much more easily have been organized on a radical appeal. But the Strike Committee were opposed in principle to any such appeal. . . .

The upshot of the matter is this: the methods of organization used in the steel strike were old-fashioned and became ostentatiously so as the organizers recognized the radical possibilities of the strike and conscientiously believed that anything other than tried trade unionism would be bad for the steel workers in their newly organized state. The cry of Bolshevism was not only a fraud on the public; it was a dangerous thing because it advertised to the mass of immigrant steel workers, who went down to defeat under old flags and old slogans, an idea and untried methods under which they might be tempted to make another battle. . . .

That the whole strike seemed extraordinarily old-fashioned to observers in England is evident from even a hasty examination of such conservative papers as the London *Times* (October 28, 1919):

The steel workers' strike, which is the rock upon which the Industrial Conference split, turns on the question of recognizing unions, *an issue which has gone into the limbo of almost forgotten things here,* as between employers and employed. . . . The

employers in America have evidently something to learn in these matters. They have been apt to compare with some complacency their own relations with labor to those existing in this country and to attribute their comparative immunity from labor troubles to the superior atmosphere of the United States or to their own superior management. It is really due to the simple fact that the Labor Movement in the United States is historically a good many years behind our own. But it will infallibly tread the same broad course with certain differences determined by local conditions, and to resist the inevitable is a great mistake. There are many different elements present in the States, and a far greater tendency to violence is one of them.

* * *

It must be clearly noted that the twelve-hour day schedules are compulsory. The Steel Corporation's "basic eight-hour day" is a method of paying wages and in no way concerns hours. The twelve-hour day workman cannot knock off at the end of eight hours, if he wants to retain his employment. Neither can he escape the eighteen-hour or twenty-four hour "turn," usually every fortnight, which goes with most of the twelve-hour day schedules. He can "take it or leave it" but he cannot bargain over his job's hours. . . .

The twelve-hour day is not a metallurgical necessity; steel masters are not caught in the grip of their gigantic machinery. . . .

The fact that the eight-hour day has replaced the twelve-hour day in England, on the Pacific Coast, in the Pueblo plant of the Colorado Fuel and Iron Co., and in some "independent" plants near Chicago and Pittsburgh, proves that it is not a matter of necessity. Metallurgists agree that production is better,—by a small percentage, but better,—on the three-shift eight-hour day. . . .

Only two excuses were offered to the Commission for the twelve-hour day; labor shortage and workmen's preference. On analysis we shall see that both are baseless and that the true causes concern much more the helplessness of disorganized immigrant labor. First, it is advisable to analyze steel production sufficiently to understand the kinds of jobs these are which must be followed twelve hours a day.

It is an epigram of the industry that "steel is a man killer." Steel workers are chiefly attendants of gigantic machines. The steel business tends to become, in the owners' eyes, mainly the machines. Steel jobs are not easily characterized by chilly scientific terms. Blast furnaces over a hundred feet high, blast "stoves" a hundred feet high, coke ovens miles long, volcanic Bessemer converters, furnaces with hundreds of tons of molten steel in their bellies, trains of hot blooms, miles of rolls end to end hurtling white hot rails along,—these masters are attended by sweating servants whose job is to get close enough to work but to keep clear enough to save limb and life. It is concededly not an ideal industry for men fatigued by long hours.

To comprehend precisely what the twelve-hour day meant, the Inquiry gathered data from steel mill officials and from the workers themselves. Mr. Gary's testimony was:

It is not an admitted fact that more than eight hours is too much for a man to labor per day. . . . I had my own experience in that regard (on a farm); and all our officers worked up from the ranks. They came up from day laborers. They were all perfectly satisfied with their time of service; they all desired to work longer hours . . . the employees generally do not want eight hours. . . . I do not want you to think that for a moment. (Senate Testimony, Vol. I, p. 180.)

Mr. H. D. Williams, president of the Carnegie Steel Company, said that he had worked fourteen hours a day and did not feel he was any the worse for it. . . .

First, what exactly is the schedule of the twelve-hour worker? Here is the transcript of the diary of an American worker, the observations of a keen man on how his fellows regard the job, the exact record of his own job and hours made in the spring of 1919, before the strike or this Inquiry, and selected here because no charge of exaggeration could be made concerning it. It begins:

Calendar of one day from the life of a Carnegie steel workman at Homestead on the open hearth, common labor:

5:30 to 12 (midnight)—Six and one-half hours of shoveling, throwing and carrying bricks and cinder out of bottom of old furnace. Very hot.

12:30—Back to the shovel and cinder, within few feet of pneumatic shovel drilling slag, for three and one-half hours.

4 o'clock—Sleeping is pretty general, including boss.

5 o'clock—Everybody quits, sleeps, sings, swears, sighs for 6 o'clock.

6 o'clock—Start home.

6:45 o'clock—Bathed, breakfast.

7:45 o'clock—Asleep.

4 P.M.—Wake up, put on dirty clothes, go to boarding house, eat supper, get pack of lunch.

5:30 P.M.—Report for work.

This is the record of the night shift; a record of inevitable waste, inefficiency and protest against "arbitrary" hours. Next week this laborer will work the day shift. What is his schedule per week? Quoting again from the diary:

Hours on night shift begin at 5:30; work for twelve hours through the night except Saturday, when it is seventeen hours, until 12 Sunday noon, with one hour out for breakfast; the following Monday ten hours;

total from 5:30 Monday to 5:30 Monday
87 *hours, the normal week.*

The Carnegie Steel worker works 87
hours out of the 168 hours in the week. Of
the remaining 81 he sleeps seven hours per
day; total of 49 hours. He eats in another
fourteen; walks or travels in the street car
four hours; dresses, shaves, tends furnace,
undresses, etc., seven hours. His one reaction
is "What the Hell!"—the universal text ac-
companying the twelve-hour day. . . .

None can dispute the demoralizing
effects on family life and community life
of the inhuman twelve-hour day. As a
matter of arithmetic twelve-hour day
workers, even if the jobs were as lei-
surely as Mr. Gary says they are, have
absolutely no time for family, for town,
for church or for self-schooling; for any
of the activities that begin to make full
citizenship; they have not the time, let
alone the energy, even for recreation. . . .

In analyzing the organization resulting
in the strike it is necessary to draw a
distinction which, however, cannot be
clearly kept throughout the discussion;
that is, the distinction between the leadership and the body of strikers. The leadership came from the organized labor
movement, the American Federation of
Labor, having comparatively few foot-
holds in the steel industry. The labor
movement initiated the organizing campaign, invited by the steel workers, according to the labor leaders, invading
where it was not wanted, according to
the employers. Both statements are correct and neither lays emphasis on the
principal fact—the isolation of the mass
of immigrant steel workers, unable to
unite their thirty nationalities, ignorant
of, or fearful of, the ways by which
workmen act to change their conditions
of labor. These steel workers are more
important than their leaders, in analyzing causes of the strike, and in this sec-

tion of the report the emphasis laid on
the leadership must be clearly grasped
as over-emphasis, due to the fact that it
is *organization* which is being analyzed.
Such analysis must begin with the list
of twenty-four participating A.F. of L.
unions, whose officers composed the National Committee for Organizing Iron
and Steel Workers, of which John Fitzpatrick, President of the Chicago Federation of Labor, became Chairman, with
William Z. Foster as Secretary-Treasurer. . . .

What made 300,000 steel workers
leave the mills on September 22nd and
stay away in greater or fewer numbers
for a period up to three and a half
months?

It cannot be too strongly emphasized
that a strike does not consist of a plan
and a call for a walkout. There has been
many a call with no resultant walkout;
there has been many a strike with no
preceding plan or call at all. Strike
conditions are conditions of mind.

The frame of mind of steel workers
in late 1918 and early 1919, first and
foremost, as detailed in other sections of
this report, grew out of their conditions
of labor, things with which Mr. Gompers, Mr. Fitzpatrick and the strike organizers had little to do. That three-
quarters of steel employees, who were
forced to work from 10 to 14 hours a
day, developed a frame of mind of more
or less chronic rebellion, largely the physical reaction from exhaustion and dep-
rivation. Rebellious reaction from having no "say" in the conduct of the job
was also chronic, though less so. These
were fundamental facts in steel workers'
minds, of which they were constantly
reminded by endless "grievances"; these
facts Mr. Foster was thinking of when
he said that if the steel companies had
shortened hours and granted some sort

of representation, "this movement would never have had a show." In this respect the Finance Committee of the U.S. Steel Corporation was the principal organizer of the strike.

This rebellious state of mind had existed a long time without a mass strike. The high labor turnover in steel plants means that thousands of steel workers have been going on "individual strikes" for several years. The "labor shortage" which steel companies experience is a persistent evidence of this "strike" frame of mind. The high rate of absenteeism is another evidence. Whetting this state of discontent were two other psychological factors, both growing out of the war and previously referred to in this report. Together they were far more important than Mr. Gompers or Mr. Foster or anybody except possibly Mr. Gary.

The first factor was the increased consideration accorded steel workers, by foremen daily and by high company officials frequently, in the course of the national war effort. The steel worker was made to feel that he was mightily helping to win the war, with his steel shells, steel guns, gun carriages, ship plates, etc., etc., etc., in short, with his maximum production. . . .

Most important of all, the Government was putting its seal of recognition on Mr. Gompers personally, and the War Labor Board was making "collective bargaining" and the "right to organize in trade and labor unions" the text of business awards. . . .

The data before the Commission show that at the beginning of the strike steel workers in great numbers had the liveliest expectation of governmental assistance in getting their organization "recognized" by the Steel Corporation. Particularly the "foreigners," with their tra-

dition of awed respect for constituted authority, talked about the government coming to the rescue; some believed "Mr. Wilson will run the mills." . . .

The second psychological factor growing out of the war, with which American labor leaders had even less to do, sprang from events in Europe. The news of two years' happenings there deeply influenced all labor, of course, but the evidence indicates peculiar influence on steel workers. English speaking workers were impressed by what happened in England; the mass of Slavic workers, constituting from 30 per cent to 70 per cent in many mills, were stirred by Russia. . . .

Communists, looking for evidence of Lenin as an organizer of the steel strike, found little to please them. Two students of Lenin's method, one a Communist enthusiast, returned from rather hasty investigations of the Pittsburgh strikers in a state of dejection. They reported that the Slavic workers "were mad enough but didn't know anything." They laid the blame to the strike leadership and to the lack of propaganda. They recommended breaking down the influence of A.F. of L. organizers, Foster especially, and "a campaign of education by leaflets." They said the steel workers were not ripe for "action" (Communist) but would be particularly ripe for "education" after the strike was lost. One of these investigators termed Fitzpatrick "a menace because he wanted to lead the workers away from economic direct action and into a labor party, to follow the losing by-path of bourgeois political action"; he considered Foster "worse than useless because his reputation as an old radical spoiled the true picture of the strike—the worst kind of an A.F. of L. strike. . . .

. . . Steel workers felt that in this period workers everywhere were moving to get rid of things which chained them—czaristic dynasties in some lands, in others slavish hours of labor and subjection to industrial machines. This is a rather more sensible view than to suppose that several hundred thousand immigrants, many of them illiterate, struck in 1919 because they had carefully read and mastered rules for forming soviets. Their intention, analysis seems to indicate, was to reach an agreement with the Steel Corporation about hours, wages and bosses, rather than to send armed workers to seize the Allegheny County court house or the Pennsylvania railroad station. What immigrant and native-born learned from Europe in 1919 was that it seemed a good time to end the autocracy which they knew—the Corporation's way of running its workers. . . .

Blacklists as an integral part of the anti-union alternative of course are ordinarily kept secret by the companies. The steel plant in Monessen, however, which freely lent its "labor file" to an investigator to study, included among the detectives' reports, etc., several blacklists. To most actual plant managers, as distinguished from Mr. Gary, blacklists seem after all too common to be deeply concealed. . . .

Two extensive labor-detective strikebreaking corporations, with offices in a dozen cities, had a hand in fighting the steel strike. Documents and reports from one of the concerns filled half the Monessen "labor file." Affidavits and documents were obtained from the other, which operated chiefly in the Chicago District. Also in the Monessen "labor file" were the reports furnished by two other "detective" agencies. In the file were the forms of contracts under which these concerns were hired and operate. Their "operatives' " reports run from the illiterate scribblings of professional parasites to the most accurate transcriptions of union locals' secret meetings. Interviews with the officers of these strikebreaking concerns gave further insight into the range of their "work" in the steel strike. A sub-report furnishes the material for building up a day by day story of the strike in Monessen. The other documents and the interviews show the extent. It is all of a piece and it is the least noble side of the war waged for the "open shop" in steel.

The manager of the detective strikebreaking corporation whose reports and contracts appeared in the Monessen "labor file," when interviewed spoke fairly freely of his concern's views and activities. He had over five hundred "operatives" at work in the steel strike. Some of his operatives had been injected into the steel plants a year before. Many of his operatives had become officers of labor unions. He said that there was on the National Strike Committee a labor leader who took his money. He denied that his concern was a mere detective or strike-breaking concern.

He used the same arguments as Mr. Gary in explaining why he supported Mr. Gary. He said workmen had a right to organize but the "open shop" must be preserved. He said that labor unions had rights but that the unions had fallen into the hands of radical leaders.

Like Mr. Gary he denied that he wanted to crush unions. . . .

Just as in this plant in Monessen where, as the superintendent and the investigator knew, two "detective agencies" had propagandist-spies mixed with the real workers, so throughout the domain of steel, watchers—from subsidized workers to hired detectives—peak and glower at the labor force and try to guess, by the way men walk or look or talk or stay silent or spit, what they are thinking.

The reach of the industrial spy system and the reliance placed on it were brought home to the Commission of Inquiry by the spy report on the Commission which was sent to Mr. Gary. It has been referred to before; the Commission in November read the report, knew that it was being distributed in the territory of the Steel Corporation's plants, and disregarded so amusingly false a document; in December when the Commission made its effort to settle the strike, Mr. Gary exhibited it and cross-examined the Commissioners on its charges. Someone had set a spy on the Commission and on the Interchurch World Movement. The anonymous "special report" was dated November 12. The Commission's first interview with Mr. Gary had been on November 10.

The "special report" names (misspelling the names) some of the Commission's investigators, names others as investigators who were not, and calls all named "radicals," "members of the I.W.W.," "Reds" and "active in the organization known as the People's Print . . . formerly known as the People's Peace Council, better known as the National Civil Liberties League." No statement made about the investigators was true. . . .

To maintain steel companies' non-union policies, communities lost their rights of assembly so completely that in some towns government agents, sent to give patriotic lectures, were denied the right to hold meetings; one such was arrested.

The extent to which rights were abrogated depended largely upon the extent to which non-unionism was endangered. If labor organizers were aggressive and local restrictive ordinances were insufficient the most arbitrary executive acts were resorted to. During the strike the repression was complete. Legally the Interchurch Commission of Inquiry being composed of "three or more persons" broke the Sheriff's orders by the simple act of assembling and "loitering" in the streets of Pittsburgh. A Commissioner conversed with strikers in the office used as their headquarters in Braddock; five minutes after his departure State troopers broke into the place demanding "that speaker" and started to close down the office because "a meeting" had been held. . . .

During the strike violations of personal rights and personal liberty were wholesale; men were arrested without warrants, imprisoned without charges, their homes invaded without legal process, magistrates' verdicts were rendered frankly on the basis of whether the striker would go back to work or not. But even these things would seem to be less a concern to the nation at large than the degradation, persistent and approved by "public opinion," of civil liberties in behalf of private concerns' industrial practices. . . .

Local magistrates, police authorities, etc., around Pittsburgh were very frequently steel mill officials or relations of mill officials. In other cases steel mill officials exercised police authority without the excuse of having been previously elected to public office. For example, besides Sheriff Haddock of Allegheny County whose brother was superintendent of an American Sheet & Tin Plate plant (Corporation subsidiary), Mayor Crawford of Duquesne was the brother of the President of the McKeesport Tin Plate Co.; President Moon of the Borough Council of Homestead was chief of the mechanical department of the Homestead mill; Burgess Lincoln of Munhall was a department superintendent in the same mill. The Burgess of Clairton was a mill official; etc., etc. When a striker was taken before mill-official public-officials he was likely to suspect connections between his fate and the steel company's desires. . . .

The charges on which strikers were arraigned before local magistrates, then imprisoned or fined, were often never recorded and never learned by the prisoners. Recorded formal specifications included "stopping men from going to work," "cursing" (the state police or deputies), "abusing," "refusing to obey orders" (to move on, etc.), "going out of his house before daylight," "laughing at the police," "throwing strike cards out on the street," "smiling at the state police." Fines ran from $10 to $50 or $60. Imprisonment terms ran up to months. Arrested men were frequently taken, not to jail, but inside the steel mill and held there. The charges of beatings, clubbings, often substantiated by doctors' and eye-witnesses' affidavits, were endless and monotonous; in most communities the only public official to appeal to turned out to be another mill official.

Federal officials' active intervention concerned chiefly (1) the Department of Justice, whose connections with steel company "under-cover men" were referred to earlier, and whose public activities dealt with raids in search of "reds" and Attorney General Palmer's statements about "reds" in the steel strike; and (2) the U.S. Army. Both cases contributed to steel workers' beliefs about strike-breaking activities. . . . Congressional intervention in the shape of the investigation and report of the Senate Committee on Labor and Education filled the strikers with a bitterness only to be understood by detailed comparison of the Committee's report and the facts.

Marshall Olds: ANALYSIS OF THE INTER-CHURCH WORLD MOVEMENT REPORT

CONSIDERING then merely the Interchurch Report itself without reference to any outside facts as to its origin or authorship, it is plain and conclusive that:

First: The Interchurch Report as a whole, and in general as to its separate and detailed conclusions is based on evidence that is plainly insufficient. The "rock-bottom evidence" of the whole Report is stated by the Report itself to consist of "500 affidavits" which are chiefly from "the mass of low-skilled foreigners." Irrespective of the value of these 500 affidavits themselves, it is hardly possible under any circumstances that 500 such affidavits could constitute adequate evidence of facts as to the point of view of 500,000 workers and as to the operation of a great basic industry.

Moreover, in specific and detailed argument throughout the Report, the evidence presented is equally inadequate, repeatedly consisting merely of some one or few isolated, dramatic incidents or allegations from which the Report immediately generalizes and draws sweeping conclusions.

Second: Chiefly because of its persistence in generalizing from insufficient evidence, the Interchurch Report is repeatedly and conspicuously self-contradictory in regard to major conclusions. For instance:

It frequently repeats the statement—as one of its main arguments for the need of "Collective Bargaining"—that the workers as a matter of practice cannot take their grievances any higher than the foreman. Yet in a majority of the evidence which the Report itself later presents, consisting of affidavits of low-skilled foreign workers in regard to specific grievances, these affidavits definitely state that these workers actually did take their grievances "from the foreman to the superintendent," or "to the main office," or "to the General Superintendent," or "to the general manager."

The Interchurch Report states, as a major conclusion, that common labor worked (1919) 74 hours a week—over 12 hours a day. It states as another major conclusion that the annual wage of steel common labor for 1919 was "under $1466 a year." As a matter of simple arithmetic, based on the known and admitted wage rate, if common labor averaged over twelve hours a day, their wages were not "under $1466 a year," but between $1700 and $1800 a year, or else common labor worked only 249 days a year which would entirely contradict the whole Interchurch argument that the industry was "speeded up in every direction"—that the workers only got a Sunday off once in 6 months, etc.

The Interchurch Report spends a major part of Chapter II arguing to the conclusion that the steel strike was not "plotted or led by reds or syndicalists

From *Analysis of the Interchurch World Movement Report on the Steel Strike* by Marshall Olds, Part II (New York, G. P. Putnam's Sons, 1922), pp. 371–378, 382, 384–385, 467–468, 470–471, 473–475.

or Bolshevists"—that it did not seek to "overthrow established leaders and established institutions of organized labor." Chapter VI, however, is devoted mainly to showing in detail that the whole unionization and strike movement was planned by, and its most important leader was, a man who has himself admitted in writing, both before and since the strike, that he was an ultra-radical working in general, and in the steel strike in particular, towards overthrowing what are at least the expressed present aims of organized labor, and he specifically refers to the Steel Strike as an example of the degree to which they are being overthrown. Moreover the authors of the Interchurch Report state plainly in this Chapter VI that they were entirely and in detail familiar with his point of view and his aims; in which chapter it is also stated that circumstances at the time of the steel strike and in general are forcing all organized labor from its present theories of "craft" unionism to the "industrial" or radical unionism for which they admit Mr. Foster is working. Moreover in this same later chapter the Interchurch Report specifically states that the two principal "psychological factors" which influenced the big majority of the "unskilled foreigners" in the strike—and it is plainly admitted that in general the unskilled foreigners were the backbone of the strike—were such radical motives as that the workers had got control of the Russian government; that they had or were about to get control of the British government; that they expected as a result of the strike that "Mr. Wilson was going to run the steel mills," etc.

On page 95 the Report states that the steel companies, in their efforts to force workers to over-exertion, made each wage raise just enough to meet the increased cost of living, yet, in a footnote on page 97, it states that earnings had gone up 150% during a period in which it is a matter of official record that the increased cost of living had gone up only half that much.

Others of the most important major conclusions and many minor conclusions throughout the Report are similarly irreconcilably contradictory.

Third: The Interchurch Report is openly and wholly an *ex parte* argument. The statement in the beginning of the Report that the scope of the inquiry was chiefly among the "mass of low-skilled foreigners," and that "the statements and affidavits of 500 (such) steel workers constituted the rock-bottom of the findings," and the repeated statements that the Interchurch Report investigators received little support or evidence from the Steel Companies constitute palpable admissions of the *ex parte* nature of the whole Report. Such admissions, however, are entirely superfluous. *The authors of the Interchurch Report had available all the evidence presented in the present analysis.* They obviously, however, not only made no effort to seek out evidence except on one side but they deliberately omitted to consider the most widely known and official facts—even facts which often form an integral part of the evidence the Report does use—whenever these facts are in any way favorable to the steel companies.

In its entire discussion of wages, the Interchurch Report attempts to prove the contrary without once mentioning the existence of the official government figures and other authoritative studies which show plainly and specifically that steel wages are by far the highest in industry, even though some of these figures are found buried away in the Appendix of the Report itself.

The whole weight of evidence in the Senate Investigation was against the strike, as both Foster and the Interchurch Report tacitly admit by their repeated condemnation of the Senate Investigation. The Interchurch Report quotes frequently and voluminously from the Senate Investigation. Yet not only does it not quote any Senate evidence whatever that is in the least favorable to the steel companies, but in the unfavorable evidence which it does quote, it carefully expurgates any statements or remarks that are favorable to the companies' side and quotes only that part which is favorable to the workers' side. . . .

Fourth: The Interchurch Report continually resorts to insinuations and to misleading language to create impressions about facts which it fails to state openly or argue on their merits.

On page 14, line 1 and elsewhere the Interchurch Report makes, merely in passing, the ambiguous criticism that "increases in wages during the war in no case were at a sacrifice of stockholders' dividends." As a matter of fact, wages were increased more than dividends. . . .

Fifth: In regard to its major conclusions, in so far as they are susceptible of being arrived at on a basis of definite fact —which includes those in regard to the most important subjects of wages, profits, hazards, the number of 12-hour workers, the nature of 12-hour work, the attitude of the companies toward the men, etc.— it has been shown specifically and in detail that the conclusions of the Interchurch Report are the opposite of the provable truth.

In regard to other major issues in the steel strike, such as the attitude of the steel workers toward their alleged grievances, toward trade union collective bargaining, in regard to the number of workers who actually struck, in regard to radicalism in the strike movement, etc., which issues, because they largely involve facts as to the opinions and points of view of large numbers of men and other complex facts or complicated circumstances, must be arrived at by a careful determination of the *weight of evidence,* it has been shown specifically and in detail that the strong weight of real evidence, which is seldom even considered by the Interchurch Report, clearly shows that the conclusions which the Interchurch Report assumes to reach are in general unwarranted and often definitely untrue. . . .

Sixth: It is obvious from the foregoing that the Interchurch Report is not, as it specifically assumes to be, and as the fact that it is signed by the Interchurch World Movement gives the impression that it should be, an impartial investigation or argument on the merits of the case, but that on the contrary it is a self-evidently inaccurate, self-contradictory and blatantly *ex parte* argument and as such not a safe textbook even for those who desire to agree with its conclusions.

Seventh: But the Interchurch Report cannot be regarded merely as an overzealous *ex parte* argument for it reaches its conclusions, which it itself frequently admits are the opposite of those held by American public opinion in general, not only through the faulty arguments and questionable methods already emphasized but repeatedly through means that are utterly indefensible on any grounds. . . .

Eighth: The publication of its second volume, including one considerable group of its "500 rock-bottom affidavits" shows that this fundamental evidence on which the Interchurch Report itself states that it is based is, at least as far as there is any basis for judging or checking it, as manipulated and falsified as the foregoing "statistics." . . .

The Interchurch Report itself admits that these "rock-bottom affidavits" were not in general composed or phrased by the men who signed them with their names or marks. It states that they were largely composed and phrased by its own investigators or by James R. Maurer, President of the Pennsylvania Federation of Labor. Mr. Maurer is a conspicuous radical who signed himself in now-published correspondence with the Russian Soviet as "representing 300 radical groups in 42 states." Of the 41 "rock-bottom affidavits" published, over 30 show dates before the Interchurch investigation began and therefore must have been secured by Mr. Maurer. . . .

Ninth: The lengths to which the Interchurch Report thus constantly goes to support its *ex parte* argument naturally raises the question as to just where that *ex parte* argument leads.

That it is in favor of the workers, and particularly the unskilled foreign workers, and their demands, is of course obvious, but it is also obvious that the Interchurch Report argument constantly goes much further than this and it is conspicuous that at least certain parts of the Report argue to certain theories and conclusions which are generally regarded as radical.

Following this lead, a careful comparison between the seven chief aims to which the Socialist, Communist, Syndicalist and other radical groups are in common committed, with the principal arguments of the Interchurch Report, shows that—in the attacks and the kind of attacks it makes on certain specific forces of law and order,—in the type of labor organization it specifically favors— in both the quantity and quality of its

argument on free speech—in the phraseology in which it words these attacks and advances these theories—and otherwise, the Interchurch Report exactly parallels official manifestos of the Communist Party and other official ultra-radical propaganda documents. Moreover with this fact established, an examination of the whole Report shows clearly that many of its arguments and conclusions are entirely incompatible with the operation of the whole modern industrial system, while, except for one conclusion in the separate "Findings," not only is no argument in the Report incompatible with radical theories and aims but all its principal arguments in regard to wages, surplus, control of industry, labor unions, social consequences are, at least as far as they go, exactly parallel to the fundamental arguments of radicalism, entirely and particularly susceptible of being quoted and used in favor of radicalism, and are as a matter of fact being so quoted and used by radicals in all parts of the country today. . . .

The Interchurch Report on the Steel Strike, signed as it is by nine prominent religious leaders and underwritten by the Interchurch World Movement, has undoubtedly been widely accepted at substantially its face value, by a large part not merely of the religious world, but also of the general public. . . .

Beyond all facts as to the merits of the Interchurch Report itself, however, or as to its use, is the fact that it is a representative document—a conspicuous typical example of a new type of propaganda which is being more and more widely used and whose motives and methods as well as whose merits should therefore at least be recognized and understood by the public. . . .

The primary effort of radicalism,—to build its active fighting minority of industrial workers through capitalizing discontent, preaching class hatred, appealing to envy and greed and maligning public officials and courts and government,—is more or less open and recognized. Its secondary effort, however, to deceive and disunite the general public, to confuse economic and political issues and to disrupt or dissipate every constructive economic effort depends for its success upon its more or less complete concealment.

For the achievement, therefore, of its secondary effort, radicalism changes its appearance and appeal—its red becomes pink or "merely liberal" and its programme of hate and plunder becomes one of "sympathy" and "idealism." In this guise radicalism has created various and widely distributed organizations to carry its propaganda to the general public. Among the most prominent of these are the Rand School of Social Science, the Bureau of Industrial Research, organized by Mr. Robert W. Bruere, a teacher of literature in the Rand School until this school was being made conspicuous through government attack. . . .

Radical "boring from within" does not, of course, mean the attempt to convert all the members of the organization subjected to this operation to the extreme of radicalism of the "borers." . . .

The radical directors of ultra-radical central organizations serve as directors and officers with less radical and even conservative directors in a much wider group of "liberal" organizations, while the most intimate of their fellow directors in such organizations in turn serve as directors or officers in a still wider group of more "merely liberal" organizations. Again we have an excellent example in the Interchurch Report itself. Mr. Foster, the hero of the Report, is a member of the No. 1 Communist governing

organization, in constant touch with Moscow. As a member of the Federated press he is in constant touch with Mr. Blankenhorn, who wrote the Interchurch Report, and Mr. Bruere, the head of its technical assistants. Blankenhorn and Bruere in turn, in their Bureau of Industrial Research, are in touch with the trade unions, social organizations, college socialist societies, and the like, to which they supply data and material. Through common membership in the National Committee of the American Civil Liberties Union, Foster is in active touch with James A. Maurer, who furnished most of the Interchurch "rock-bottom" affidavits, and Maurer in turn is president of the Pennsylvania State Federation of Labor, a subordinate organization of the American Federation of Labor. Through the same organization Foster is in touch with Baldwin, whose assistants are seeking from the courts a new interpretation of the principles of free speech, of the press, and of assemblage, which will destroy the power of the Government to protect itself and its citizens against propaganda for the overthrow of our government by force and violence.

Through its control, thus secured and maintained and directed, of an ever increasing number of organizations, which profess to represent, and are accepted by the general public as representing, some religious or broadly social work, radicalism is today carrying on an "under cover" propaganda campaign which is as far reaching as it is generally unsuspected. . . .

That the Interchurch Report is typical of this general radical "under-cover" propaganda with which, in all manner of disguises, the country is today being broadcast, is plain from the comparison of arguments, conclusions and even phraseology already made, and from the fact that it was actually prepared by the representatives of the same organizations which are at least ultimately responsible for this general campaign. But the Interchurch Report is more than merely typical. From its inception, in which the radicals had such a prominent part, the Interchurch Steel Strike Report offered the possibilities of having their "undercover" propaganda underwritten and circulated by what promised to be the most influential religious organization in American history. The "borers" in this case consisted not merely of the immediate representatives of one particular radical group, as is usual, but of some of the ablest representatives of the most important interlocking radical groups. Their success was such that they had the preparation of the Report substantially in their own hands. . . .

Suggestions for Additional Reading

An excellent history of labor relations in the steel industry is that of R. R. R. Brooks, *As Steel Goes, . . .* (Yale University Press, New Haven, 1950). Other general volumes on labor history which contain chapters on the steel industry include Selig Perlman and Philip Taft, *History of Labor in the United States, 1896–1932*, Chapters XIV and XXXV (Macmillan, New York, 1935), Samuel Yellen, *American Labor Struggles* Chapter VIII (Harcourt, Brace, New York, 1936), and Norman J. Ware, *Labor in Modern Industrial Society*, Chapter 17 (D. C. Heath, Boston, 1935).

Insights into housing, living standards, working conditions, and the social environment of steel workers in the Pittsburgh area a few years before the 1919 strike are afforded by the six volumes edited by Paul U. Kellogg entitled *The Pittsburgh Survey*, published by the Russell Sage Foundation between 1910 and 1914. Of these, John A. Fitch, *The Steel Workers* (New York, 1911), deals most directly with conditions in the steel mills, although the other volumes give significant insights into the setting of the 1919 conflict. These are: *The Pittsburgh District: Civic Frontage* (New York, 1914), *Wage-Earning Pittsburgh* (New York, 1914), *Women and the Trades* (New York, 1909), *Work-Accidents and the Law* (New York, 1910), *Homestead, The Households of a Mill Town* (New York, 1910). A perceptive account of the impact of mechanical evolution on labor types employed in the steel industry is given by Charles Reitell in *The Journal of Political Economy*, Volume 26, pp. 274–290, March 1918.

The viewpoint of the U.S. Steel Corporation in the 1919 strike is sympathetically presented by Arundel Cotter, *United States Steel—The Corporation with a Soul* (Doubleday, Garden City, New York, 1921). Something of the same eulogistic attitude permeates the biography by Ida M. Tarbell, *The Life of Elbert H. Gary, A Story of Steel* (D. Appleton and Co., New York, 1925) (note especially Chapter 11).

A militant stand against the labor policies of the steel companies is taken by Horace B. Davis in his *Labor and Steel* (International Publishers, New York, 1933) and by Louis Adamic, *Dynamite: The Story of Class Violence in America* (Harper & Bros., 1931), Chapter 27. In the latter volume, the moral is drawn that nonviolence has proved an inadequate weapon of strike strategy.

The two basic source books on the steel dispute of 1919 include the hearings of the Senate Committee and the investigations of the Interchurch World Movement. Three volumes of hearings and conclusions were published by the United States Senate, Sixty-sixth Congress: *Hearings before the Committee on Education and Labor, U.S. Senate, Sixty-sixth Congress, Pursuant to S. Res. 202* (Government Printing Office, Washington, 1919), *Hearings before the Committee on Education and Labor, U.S. Senate, Sixty-sixth Congress, Pursuant to S. Res. 188* (Government Printing Office, Washington, 1919), and *Investigation of Strike in*

Steel Industries, Hearings before the Committee on Education and Labor, United States Senate, Sixty-sixth Congress, First Session, Pursuant to S. Res. 188 and S. Res. 202, Part 2 (Government Printing Office, Washington, 1919). Divergent conclusions were reached in the two volumes published by the Interchurch World Movement, *Report on the Steel Strike of 1919* and *Public Opinion and the Steel Strike* (Harcourt, New York, 1920 and 1921).

Each of these efforts to assemble direct evidence concerning the strike and to reach an impartial conclusion concerning it brought forth an answer. Marshall Olds in 1922 published his *Analysis of the Interchurch World Movement Report on the Steel Strike* (G. P. Putnam's Sons, New York, 1922), which was widely distributed by the steel companies. It constituted an indictment of the impartiality and accuracy of the Interchurch effort. William Z. Foster, in his *The Great*

Steel Strike and Its Lessons (B. W. Heubsch, New York, 1920), vigorously takes issue with the conclusions of the Senate Committee report and upholds the Interchurch findings.

For an assessment of the financial history of the steel industry see Walter Adams, editor, *The Structure of American Industry* (Macmillan, 1961), and H. R. Seager and Charles A Gulick, Jr., *Trust and Corporation Problems* (Harper & Bros., New York, 1929), Chapter 13. The latter includes an excellent account of the development of the U.S. Steel Corporation.

To observe the treatment accorded the steel strike in the press, a reading of newspapers and magazines of the period is recommended. This issue is treated in detail in *Public Opinion and the Steel Strike,* mentioned above. Other glimpses may be obtained in *The Literary Digest,* Volume 63, and in the newspapers of the time.

2 3 4 5 6 7 8 9 10

W